MIND YOUR MONEY

MIND YOUR MONEY

Insightful Stories and
Strategies to Help You
Reach Your #MoneyGoals

YANELY ESPINAL

LIONCREST
PUBLISHING

MIND YOUR MONEY
Insightful Stories and Strategies to Help You Reach Your #MoneyGoals

FIRST EDITION

ISBN   978-1-5445-1655-4   *Hardcover*
        978-1-5445-1654-7   *Paperback*
        978-1-5445-1653-0   *Ebook*
        978-1-5445-1656-1   *Audiobook*

For Mami, Papi, and the Espinal family.

*Gracias por los valores que me han enseñado,
sobre todo el servicio a los demás.*

*Thank you for the values you've instilled in
me, especially being of service to others.*

For Jamil Abreu.

*Grateful for our trips,
and hammock naps together.
My partner for life.*

Contents

PART 1

—

IT'S ALL IN YOUR HEAD

UPGRADE YOUR MONEY MINDSET

CHAPTER 1

Shhh! Don't Talk about Money

"WHERE'S MAMI?!" I HEARD MY SISTER YELL OUT THE window. I stopped sweeping the tiny concrete slab we New Yorkers call a backyard and yelled back just as loudly.

"I don't know! She left like five minutes ago!"

Then it hit me. Mami said she had a "fetch-oh-fay" at the welfare office.

Now, if you're scrunching your brows in confusion at "fetch-oh-fay," don't worry because it took me decades to realize what the heck my mom meant. In her thick Dominican accent, she was saying "face-to-face": an in-person appointment she needed to attend at least once a year to continue receiving food stamps.

"Oh yeah!" I yelled back to my sister from the yard. "Mami had a welfare appointment!"

In Bushwick, Brooklyn, where I grew up, kids ran up and down the street while playing and everyone yelled. You might've forgotten your keys, so you'd yell to the second-floor window for someone to toss them down. Or maybe it was time to go in for dinner, so your little brother yelled from up the block, "Mami said stop playing and come inside to eat!"

That's why nine-year-old me didn't think *anything* of screaming about my mother's welfare appointment. But my older sister thought otherwise. She called me inside the house and knocked me on the top of my head as I walked through the door. "Why you gotta yell out our business like that for the whole block to hear? You tellin' everybody that Mami's on welfare! Are you stupid?" I was too young to understand exactly why she was so upset, but I did know welfare had something to do with money.

This memory is crystal clear in my mind because opening my mouth got me a *chichón*—a big ol' lump on my head—but also because it was my introduction to the idea that being on welfare was something I should be embarrassed about or ashamed of.

Shhh! Don't talk about money. Don't talk about what we have or don't have, or what we need. It's personal. It's private. It's taboo.

In hindsight, it's hilarious that my sister was so concerned with hiding the fact that we were on welfare, because most of our neighbors were on it too! If you take a walk down Bushwick Avenue today, you might come across some art galleries, juice bars, and hipster restaurants. But back in the '90s, they were bodegas, barber shops, and check-cashing spots serving low-income families who'd recently immigrated from the Caribbean.

While in line for groceries at Key Food, I saw everybody and their momma using government-issued EBT cards—it wasn't just us. I never had to pay for a beef patty at the school cafeteria, but neither did my friends. We all got free breakfast and lunch because of our parents' low-income status. For some of my friends, school lunch was the only food they could depend on eating during the week. Imagine the look of confusion on my little face when I watched cartoons or read chapter books in which the bully character yelled, "Gimme your lunch money!" I thought, *What the heck is "lunch money"?*

If your family is anything like mine, your parents didn't have much financial knowledge to pass on. Why? Because *their* parents didn't teach *them* much about personal finance. And don't even get me started on the lack of personal finance education in schools! At the time of this writing, only one out of four American high school students is required to take a full-semester personal finance class before crossing the graduation stage. For low-income students like me, the number drops to *one out of twenty!*[1]

These stats pose a huge problem, because if we don't learn about and discuss money early on, we tend to repeat familial cycles of debt and struggle.[2] Even worse, we may unintentionally pass down negative money habits to future generations.[3] One study of college students showed that having parents who avoided talking about money predicted problematic credit card use...#storyofmylife.[4]

---

1   Next Gen Personal Finance, *NGPF's 2022 State of Financial Education Report*, 2022, 4–5, https://d3f7q2msm2165u.cloudfront.net/aaa-content/user/files/2022/Annual%20Report/ NGPFAnnualReport_2022.pdf.

2   Jill M. Norvilitis and Michael G. MacLean, "The Role of Parents in College Students' Financial Behaviors and Attitudes," *Journal of Economic Psychology* 31, no. 1 (February 2010): 55–63, https://doi. org/10.1016/j.joep.2009.10.003.

3   "Parents Are Likely to Pass Down Good and Bad Financial Habits to Their Kids," T. Rowe Price, March 23, 2017, https://www.troweprice.com/corporate/en/press/t--rowe-price--parents-are-likely- to-pass-down-good-and-bad-finao.html.

4   Norvilitis and MacLean, "The Role of Parents in College Students' Financial Behaviors and Attitudes."

These patterns keep money in the hands of those fortunate enough to have received a high-quality financial education or those determined enough to figure it out on their own, like I did. Many others just can't catch a financial break.

THE SCHOOL OF HARD KNOCKS

As a low-income kid growing up in New York City, I rarely ventured more than ten blocks from home. We couldn't afford to take vacations together as a family of eleven. It was practically impossible for Mami to find affordable childcare for multiple children at once, so she stayed home with us.

As the sole breadwinner, Papi worked six days a week at an Italian restaurant. Even with government assistance in the form of food stamps, we lived paycheck to paycheck. Every dollar Papi earned went toward what we needed: rent, bills, gas, clothes, shoes, or school supplies. If a few dollars were left, he bought a lottery ticket or two. Money just wasn't the kind of thing we discussed over dinner.

To be honest, I was *afraid* to ask my parents for money. I didn't want to add to their burden. Every now and then I asked, "Papi, can I get $10 to buy French fries and pizza after school?" If I was lucky, he gave me $5. So, at twelve years old, I started making some questionable choices. At the corner bodega, I stuffed potato chips into my coat pockets and slipped ice cream sandwiches up my sleeve. Afterward, I shared them with my little friends. Luckily, my career as a snack thief was derailed by a security guard at the Duane Reade store on Knickerbocker Avenue.

Our church had a holiday gift swap that winter, and I was responsible for getting a gift for my godsister, Josefina. My problem was that I only had $4 to spend. Walking up and down the aisles, I kept eyeing a lip gloss on sale for $3.99, but I knew it would be out of my budget once they hit me with the sales tax. So, I decided to just *take* one.

Of all the lip glosses I examined, one in particular had lipstick at the top and lip gloss at the bottom. Hidden right in the middle compartment was a built-in lip liner! It had everything a girl needs to make her lip gloss poppin'. I tore off the plastic wrapper with the barcode and slipped that gloss right up my sleeve. I thought I was so smooth.

While trying to casually exit the store with my clueless sister, Tita (sorry, sis), an unassuming, portly man in a white polo shirt stopped us. "Oh, so you got tricks up ya sleeve?" We were led to the back of the store, where he played video footage of me stealing the lip gloss. That was embarrassing, but the real guilt and shame set in when I saw the looks on my parents' faces.

The following year, I applied to high school. I had my heart set on attending LaGuardia, a specialized public school offering a split school day of academics and visual or performing arts. My parents were hesitant to allow me to take the subway into Manhattan all by myself. I begged them daily and promised to redeem myself by getting straight A's. After a few long weeks, they finally agreed. I never considered stealing anything again.

Every weekday, I woke up at 6:00 a.m. to meet my friends Quiana and Jade at the subway station by 7:15 a.m. We commuted for ninety minutes on two or three different train lines to get to school on time. On many days, I arrived even earlier in order to get free tutoring in subjects where I struggled, like physics and AP calculus.

As cool as it was to swipe that white and green student

MetroCard, it didn't feel cool not having cash for a bacon-egg-and-cheese in the morning or dollar pizza after school. That's when, at fourteen, I decided to make my own money. I pulled a job application off the bulletin board in the Art Department and began my paid internship at an architecture firm a few weeks later. I was paid a minimum wage of $6 per hour and that was just enough to cover French fries, dollar pizza, and the occasional Oreo McFlurry.

My train rides home from work were spent doing homework, studying, and working on extra credit assignments. I was playing zero games with my academics, and I was determined to go above and beyond for my parents. Remember, they were aware of my petty theft situation, so I felt I had a lot to make up for. I lived this way every day until I turned eighteen, and then everything changed.

On April 2, 2007, I ran to the front stoop to pick up a stack of mail. Four months earlier, I had mailed my college applications. My teachers all told me to keep a close eye on the mail for acceptance letters, and the bigger the envelope, the better the news. I noticed the biggest envelope, at the very bottom, had my name on it. The sender? Brown University. That's right, your girl was accepted to one of the most prestigious schools in the country!

More important for me, it was one of few that offered need-blind admissions. My admission was based on merit, and due to my family's low-income status I was offered a full scholarship. Well, not exactly *full*. The scholarship covered tuition, dorm fees, and cafeteria meals. Paying for textbooks and coming up with spending money were my responsibility.

I stepped on campus and immediately applied for a job at the pizzeria. Weekly paychecks averaged about $100, so I picked up extra hours between classes and on weekends. Eventually, I took on a few more jobs in my free time including event programming, tutoring, and being a resident advisor. Juggling classes, work, and my social life wasn't as easy in college as it had been in high school. It felt like I never had enough money, no matter how many hours I worked.

As I crossed campus after a work shift one day, a woman holding a clipboard approached me and asked if I was interested in a student credit card. As a bonus, I'd get a free T-shirt after I completed the application. This was before the Credit Card Act of 2009, which prohibits credit card companies from offering gifts to students in exchange for applications.[5]

My excellent credit score today is partly due to establishing credit at eighteen years old (we'll discuss this in Chapter 4). However, at that young age, I lacked the self-control to stop using and abusing my card. Being surrounded by classmates from wealthier families, combined with not having Mami or Papi nearby to tell me "que no," led me to go buck-wild.

Picture me strutting across campus wearing $200 UGG boots, carrying an $1,800 MacBook in a $150 Coach bag, thinking I was cute. But do you know what wasn't cute? I was hiding more than $10,000 of debt from my family and friends. Do you know what was even less cute? I had no idea how much I owed because I didn't even keep track.

I needed textbooks—*swipe*. I needed that MacBook— *swipe*. I even convinced myself I needed new shoes and a dress to go partying every weekend—*swipe, swipe, swipe!*

With no understanding of how a credit card works, I was out swiping like Swiper the Fox—only I didn't have a little friend like Dora the Explorer to yell, "Swiper, no swiping!"

---

5   Credit CARD Act of 2009, Pub. L. No. 111-24, 123 Stat. 1734 (2009).

My first student credit card had a $1,500 spending limit. For some people that might sound like nothing, but to a first-gen, low-income kid from the hood, it was *everything*! I'd never had that much money before, and I didn't know how to handle myself. By the end of my senior year in the spring of 2011, I had racked up more than *$15,000* in high-interest-rate credit card debt. Plus, I owed another $6,000 in student loans to cover my study abroad program.

After graduation, I moved back home with my parents. I joined a prestigious teaching program, called Teach For America, and became an elementary school teacher. With a steady paycheck, I experienced a completely different version of New York City than the one I had known as a child. Every two weeks, when that direct deposit hit, I had opportunity and access! Just one hour on the subway and I'd be at some of the world's best rooftop bars, museums, Broadway shows, movie screenings, comedy nights, bottomless brunches, and of course Yankees games!

My annual income as a teacher in 2012 was about $41,000, so I made about $1,200 after taxes for each pay period. Again, for some that might seem scant. But in my mind, I had enough money to do whatever I wanted. I was itching to leave Mami and Papi's house and live on my own. *Alexa, play "Grown Woman" by Beyoncé.*

My mistake was not taking into account that my income needed to be higher than my spending! After paying for rent, transportation, credit card bills, utilities, my cell phone, groceries, clothes, shoes, late night taxi rides home, and helping my parents with some of their expenses from time to time, my accounts were depleted. I was getting smacked with overdraft fees almost every month.

The thought of adding up my credit card balances and

really examining my financial situation left me scared, but I could only keep up the cycle of being broke for so long. In 2013, I finally put on my big girl pants and typed the numbers into a spreadsheet. The total was just over $20,000, which scared me even more. I owed about half of what I was making annually.

How did I let it get so bad? More important, how the heck was I going to pay it all back? I went to a freaking Ivy League school but was barely scraping by, living paycheck to paycheck like my parents had. They sacrificed everything so I could have more opportunities, and what had changed? Diddly-squat!

Suddenly, I felt overwhelmed by the debt and couldn't hold back my tears. I had a life-changing choice to make: either I fix my finances, or I perpetuate the cycle of poverty.

IT'S NOT YOUR FAULT

Maybe you're feeling just as overwhelmed by debt right now. Maybe you want to save more money, but you're not sure how or where to begin. Or maybe you just started a new job and asked your Human Resources manager for help understanding the 401(k) plan, but they said they couldn't help you:

"I can't give you advice on how to complete this paperwork, sorry. You should talk to your family about it or meet with a financial professional."

But nobody in your family knows anything about 401(k) plans, so you frantically try to make sense of cryptic Google search results at midnight. *No—just, no.* Who has the time or patience to sift through millions of results with a bunch of confusing financial terms that make no sense? Why do these financial writers assume every reader has the same basic knowledge of how money works? I couldn't possibly be the only one at my job checking Wikipedia the day we got our benefits paperwork.

I remember thinking, *What the heck is a mutual fund? Is it like a mutual friend? I don't want to share my paycheck with someone else. I need this money! Forget this stupid packet. I'll just go watch* Modern Family *reruns.*

Clearly, I'm in my feelings about the financial traumas I've experienced. My point is, I was a straight-A student with a master's degree, and I had no idea how to manage money when I started adulting. Not my fault! Perhaps you've felt lost when it comes to managing money or thought, *Ugh, finance is complicated, and it's meant for rich people anyway!* Trust me—it's not your fault, either. I'm not just saying that to let people off the hook or to paint myself as a victim. When someone has gone to school for almost twenty years but has yet to learn basic money management, there's something fishy going on.

You might think I'm putting too much emphasis on what we didn't learn in school—after all, we've got the internet and can learn anything we want from our phones, right? Excellent point, so thanks for bringing that up! Unfortunately, people aren't aware of what they *don't know.* Chances are, by the time they search "how to get out of debt," they're already in debt! I know this because it happened to me. I consulted Dr. Google only after my debt became too big and scary to ignore.

Although I found what I needed to solve my money problems—blogs, videos, books, and podcasts about personal finance—I really could have used preventative care through financial education before I turned eighteen and accumulated tens of thousands of dollars in credit card debt. Don't get me wrong, I learned a lot from online research, and I'm beyond grateful for all the informative content I've come across. But it's much more difficult to dig yourself out of a hole than it is to avoid falling into one in the first place.

After the Great Recession of 2008, everyone was talking about money. It was easy to find online content about a wide variety of financial topics. The challenge was finding something that felt relatable to me as a twentysomething, Brooklyn-bred Latina with a healthy dash of sass. Almost no one who created financial books, blogs, videos, and podcasts looked like me—and they *definitely* didn't talk like me.

I didn't see my family's experiences with money reflected in mainstream financial media. Mami never had the luxury to "pay yourself first." She always had to set aside funds to send to the Dominican Republic to help support my tias and tios (aunts and uncles) who live there. Year after year I watched her put her family first, even when times were tough. My siblings and I helped her stuff giant cardboard boxes with clothes, shoes, canned food, hairspray, and all sorts of other goods to ship overseas for our cousins. We watched Mami struggle to stretch her dollars far enough to reach the Caribbean.

The term for this is "remittances." It refers to the money or goods immigrants send back to their families and friends in their home countries. I only learned this term because major news sources reported a sharp decline in remittances at the start of the pandemic in 2020.[6] No books, videos, or blogs about money mentioned this as an issue because it

---

6   Luis Noe-Bustamante, "Amid COVID-19, Remittances to Some Latin
     American Nations Fell Sharply in April, then Rebounded," Pew Research
     Center, August 31, 2020, https://www.pewresearch.org/fact-tank/2020/08/31/
     amid-covid-19-remittances-to-some-latin-american-nations-fell-sharply-in-april-then-rebounded/.

isn't included in mainstream depictions of the typical American budget. Much of the financial advice I came across straight-up clashed with money lessons I had gotten at home. Diving into personal finance felt like I was taking a class led by a professor who just didn't get me.

Okay, so what's the big deal? Students take classes they don't like all the time. Besides, most people agree financial stuff is unbearably boring. But the ways in which communities I come from continue to be excluded from personal finance empowerment speaks to bigger patterns of exclusion.

Studies show that a lack of representation can impact us negatively and affect our learning.[7] Girls and women see mostly *men* talking on television and in other media about business. People of color see mostly *white people* on major news networks discussing stock market trends. Teenagers see mostly *"old people"* in retirement ads. My fellow financial educator, author of *Money Out Loud*, Berna Anat (a.k.a. HeyBerna, my bae from the Bay), likes to say that personal finance is "hella male and hella pale."[8]

My issue has always been that it's also way too stale! To be clear, I don't think older white men in personal finance are to blame for anything. They're trying to do the same thing as I am: pass down knowledge to help others live a more financially secure life. Real talk though, when an industry has been dominated by a certain type of person, others who don't

7   Thomas S. Dee, "Teachers, Race, and Student Achievement in a Randomized Experiment," *The Review of Economics and Statistics* 86, no. 1 (February 2004): 195–210, https://doi.org/10.1162/003465304323023750; Seth Gershenson et al., *The Long-Run Impacts of Same-Race Teachers: IZA DP No. 10630* (Bonn, Germany: IZA Institute of Labor Economics, March 2017), http://dx.doi.org/10.2139/ssrn.2940620.

8   Anat, Berna, *Money Out Loud: Living Boldly, Generously, and True to You* (New York: Harper Business, 2022).

look or act like them feel excluded, and therefore unwelcome (even if they are welcome).

Too many people doubt themselves when it comes to money. The predominance of male, pale, and stale voices in the financial industry doesn't help! Their unfamiliar sayings and complex words just don't resonate with everyone. They most definitely did not resonate with me. I once heard a man on television say that to prepare for a recession American families should "make sure to have significant cash reserves." Who talks like that? Why couldn't he just say, "Make sure to save up a lot of cash"?

For most people, financial jargon makes simple concepts come off as unnecessarily confusing. So, it all begins to feel like a giant conspiracy, you know? It's like all this money stuff is made deliberately complicated for a reason, as if some people are meant to be excluded. I've felt like that, and I hated it. If I had to guess, I'd say you've probably felt that way too.

#MONEYGOALS

I've got good news and bad news to share. I'll start with the bad news: humans are hardwired for negativity.[9] We're biased toward negative information, emotions, events, and self-talk. Our psychology tends to lean toward focusing on the negative aspects of our finances, such as a low credit score, outstanding debt, or poor investment choices. The good news is that we're also hardwired for connection with others. Scientist Matthew Lieberman wrote a whole book

---

9   Amrisha Vaish, Tobias Grossmann, and Amanda Woodward, "Not All Emotions Are Created Equal: The Negativity Bias in Social-Emotional Development," *Psychological Bulletin* 134, no. 3 (May 2008): 383–403, https://doi.org/10.1037/0033-2909.134.3.383.

about this titled *Social: Why Our Brains Are Wired to Connect*. He explains that humans crave connection as much as we crave food and water. That explains why the vast majority of Americans use social media!

During my debt repayment journey, posting my #moneygoals on social media helped me stay motivated. While I encountered plenty of trolls and jerks along the way, I still got major benefits from tapping into the power of social connection. Following popular hashtags in the personal finance space helped me find posts from people all over the world and even some who lived nearby. It also helped me find more diverse voices in the space, confirming my idea that money management can look and sound different based on culture.

A few hashtags I love, some of which have millions of posts, include these and others: #moneygoals, #personalfinance, #financialliteracy, #financialempowerment, #debtfreejourney, and #savingschallenge. For a more extensive list of my top recommended hashtags and personal finance creators to follow on social media, download the free guide that pairs with this book at mindyourmoneybook.com.

My #moneygoals were simple: stick to a budget and pay off my debt. Constant visions of living a stress-free life and having extra money to blow crossed my mind. Later, I learned the proper term for extra money is "discretionary income." I didn't pray often, but when I did, I prayed for some discretionary income. I cut down on takeout orders, stopped buying new sneakers every month, and set a budget tighter than my cousin Nena's pants—I was on my grind.

But don't get it twisted. Cutting down on spending was only one part of the equation. All the money experts said I had to earn more money in order to reach my goals faster and to invest for building wealth. But this was not easy! After teaching a roomful of thirty rambunctious eight-year-olds, I typically dragged my feet home exhausted. One or two week-nights after work, and sometimes on weekends, I attended classes for my master's program. Rarely did I have the time or energy to cook, clean, visit friends and family, date, have a beauty routine, or review my finances. I had to get creative about increasing my income in ways that didn't require too much of my time. So, I sold secondhand items from my closet on multiple apps, tutored students after school, and even threaded eyebrows!

At a family party, my sisters roasted me because my eye-brows were a little too close and friendly. I love Frida Kahlo, but it's just not the look I was going for. I knew my eyebrows needed some work, but I didn't have the *discretionary* funds for eyebrow waxing. I had just sent my monthly payments to the credit card companies, and the money in my checking account was exactly what I needed until my next paycheck hit.

I had promised myself I wouldn't use my credit cards until they were completely paid off. I was just beginning my financial journey, so I was serious about showing dis-cipline and starting off strong. If I didn't have enough cash and it wasn't a true emergency, it would have to wait. Then I remembered this girl from college who threaded her own eyebrows. I thought, *If she could do that, then why can't I?* Don't worry. This is not a horror story about ripping my eyebrows off my face. I promise everything worked out.

After searching "how to thread your own eyebrows," I spent hours watching YouTube tutorials and practicing on my upper lip with an old spool of thread. I threaded my own eyebrows that night. It was painful but worth it. Yup! Hours of devouring YouTube videos saved me $12 on eyebrow threading. The real beauty of this story is that I solidified the character traits that make me who I am today: creativity, determination, and self-teaching.

Since then, I've threaded my eyebrows *hundreds* of times and have done them for Mami, my sisters, and my sister-in-law dozens of times as well. Those tutorials saved us a lot more than $12! Aside from that, I began charging my friends for eyebrow threading as another easy source of income. Hey, every little bit helps!

After being bitten by the DIY bug, I acquired new skills to affect other aspects of my spending. I bought a sewing machine for $90 and learned to make dresses, curtains, and purses from craft store fabrics. For a little while, I even sold my projects on Etsy. Oh, you didn't know? I'm a financial educator, author, and DIY queen!

I became debt-free in 2015, after making monthly payments of about $1,200 for eighteen months straight. Luckily, I experienced no major emergencies during that time, so I was able to stick to my aggressive debt payoff plan. After submitting my final payment, I wanted to get on top of the tallest mountain and scream, "I just paid off all of my debt and it changed my life!"

Instead of a mountaintop, I went to YouTube and posted videos about what I was learning and how I had paid off my debt. Millions of people have watched the videos on my channel, called MissBeHelpful. From the beginning, I preferred creating videos over blogging or writing a book. Whenever I wanted to learn something, I looked it up on YouTube, and my family, friends, and coworkers did the same. As soon as I created my channel, I posted links on Facebook and emailed my family and friends, asking them to check out my videos.

Pretty soon my audience grew beyond my close community—my videos were getting thousands of views. Emails and DMs came in from people all over the world saying they saved more money, paid off debt, and improved their credit scores. This was truly unexpected and indescribable! So many people told me that after watching my videos, they thought, *If this girl can do it, maybe I can too!*

That's exactly how I wanted people to feel about my videos. To be clear, it's not the information I share that makes them feel this way—it's how I share it. In the words of Cardi B, "I'm just a regular, degular, shmegular girl."

You won't catch me trying to impress anyone with complicated financial terms. My mission is to deter as many people as possible from repeating my money mistakes. As much as I now know about managing my finances, those who have been following me since 2015 know that I understand what it's like to be a financial hot mess.

YOUR LITTLE SOURCE OF HOPE

Are you ready to learn how to set and reach your #moneygoals—without being bored to death in the process? Don't worry, I've got you. This book is designed to be your little source of hope. Feeling hopeless about money is more common than many people realize. Just look up "financial anxiety," which is a very real thing!

As you already know, my first choice was to make videos about my money journey and not to become a writer. Then I received countless messages from supporters, viewers, and subscribers encouraging me to write a book, so here we are! This book will do two things for you: (1) plant the belief in your mind that there's potential for growth and improvement in your financial future, and (2) show you some invaluable strategies for getting there.

This isn't a one-size-fits-all guide. Too many books promise you'll be "debt-free in eight weeks" or financially successful by following "three simple steps." I'm sorry, but there's no cookie-cutter path to financial stability. Those kinds of books sell because people believe that by reading them, all their money problems will disappear. Nope!

One-plan-fits-all instructions work only if your personality and financial situation happen to align with them. So, what about the rest of us? Many end up frustrated and quit too early. To reach your #moneygoals, you must design a plan that fits your *specific circumstances*. This process requires deep reflection, time, planning, reworking the plan, and effectively executing the plan. I know that's less exciting than a gimmick, but beware of gimmicks! The world of money is full of people trying to sell you something: e-books, exclusive online courses, community memberships, and—*ooh, ooh*—don't forget about the merch!

Don't get me wrong. I respect the hustle. Maybe you've heard the saying: "Don't hate the player, hate the game." But personal finance education should be about helping people thrive financially, not spend unnecessarily. Everybody (even the financial hustler) needs to eat, so I get it. But for real, for real—I'm not looking to get rich from giving advice. I have solid investment plans in place, and I want everyone to do the same for themselves.

To me, financial education is a social justice issue. That's why instead of working in finance, I dedicated my career to education. One of my greatest accomplishments was being involved in changing laws to include high school personal finance as a required class in several states, including Florida, where I've resided since 2021. Teaching personal finance in schools helps level the playing field for all students, regardless of where they're from or where they're going.

Creating this book is also an accomplishment I'll forever be proud of, but I'm not out here *just talking about* what I've done or plan to do. Beyoncé said it best in her viral commencement speech as part of YouTube's "Dear Class of 2020" online event: "Don't talk about what you're gonna do. Don't just dream about what you're gonna do. Don't criticize somebody else for what they're not doing. You be it, be about it. Be about that action and go do it."

The greatest compliment I could get about this book would be if someone were to say, "Your book gave me hope that I can make real change, and now I'm teaching my family and community to do the same." Doesn't that make the tiny hairs on your arms and the back of your neck stand up? I want to inspire you to be an agent of change for yourself and those around you who need and deserve financial empowerment. But to get your money right, you have to first get your mind right, so that's where we'll start.

CHAPTER 2

Get Your Mind Right

YOU KNOW THAT SCENE IN EVERY ROMANTIC MOVIE when soft music plays and someone has a glowy filter around them like an angel? That was my vibe when I laid eyes on my sister's brand-new pair of Jordans. Sitting perfectly still under her bed, those white and black leather sneakers with tiny metallic accents whispered for me to put them on, like Frodo's ring.

It was late morning on a weekday. Normally I would've been at school by then, but I had a doctor's appointment scheduled that day. I felt so lucky to sleep in a little longer than the rest of my siblings, who had all left for school. I felt even luckier when I noticed my sister hadn't worn her new sneakers. This was the perfect opportunity to sneakily wear her Jordans to school so all my little classmates could see me in them! My plan was to wear them to the doctor and then beg Mami to take me to school afterward, even if only a few class periods were left.

Mami was furious because I waddled like a penguin all the way to the bus stop. I walked extra slowly because I didn't want to crease my sister's new Jordans. Not only would that reveal that I'd worn her sneakers behind her back, but she'd be fuming mad at me for making her brand-new kicks look worn out. Rather than tying the laces up, I tucked them in, which made the sneakers fit loosely around my feet.

Every time I took a step, a sneaker nearly slipped off my foot. I was determined to make it work because at my school, we had to wear a daily uniform of gray bottoms with a white shirt, but there were no rules about footwear. All the popular kids wore Nike, Adidas, Converse, and Puma. To this day the only brand, besides Jordan, that epitomizes urban NYC footwear is Timberland, which we New Yorkers call "Timbs."

For Christmas, I begged for a pair of beef and broccolis (brown and green Timbs). Instead, I got new Skechers and a pair of not-so-New Balance hand-me-downs. My parents just couldn't afford the more popular, name-brand sneakers, but my sister Tita could. She'd gotten her working papers at fourteen, and had a paid internship at a local college. You'd better believe she blew her first paycheck on a $200 pair of Jordans. I envied her for knowing what it was like to share a collective identity with the popular kids. That's why I was willing to risk it all.

When Mami and I left the doctor's office, she told me I didn't have to go to school if I didn't want to. She wanted to go straight home and start making dinner early. She even offered me an extra hour of TV. I did love me some MTV and BET, but I had a master plan! My heart almost pounded right out of my chest, and I blurted, "No, no, no. *I have to*—I mean, I want to go to school."

Confused, Mami replied, "Okay, cálmate." (Calm down.) My plan was working, but the sneakers were so wobbly that on my way down the hall to my last class, I tripped and fell flat on my face. So much for not creasing the sneakers! Everyone in the hallway burst out laughing, and now instead of a scene from a romantic movie, this was straight out of a horror flick. I was mortified. It was one of the most embarrassing moments of my childhood. I'll never forget the names and faces of the kids who laughed at me. You know who you are: Charles, Michael, and Nicole!

Too humiliated to sit through class and do any actual learning, I cried my way to the nurse's office. The nurse called my mom to come pick me up. Mami was so angry with me for inconveniencing her. Tita was also mad at me for creasing her Jordans, but I felt pretty freaking good inside. I saw kids laughing at me, but before that I saw them see me walk down the hall wearing brand-new Jordans. Even though it was fleeting, I had felt the bulletproof confidence of being cool, and it was worth all the drama.

At the time, I didn't know what was going on in my brain that could lead me to do something so ridiculous. I didn't even find it ridiculous! As a matter of fact, it happened again in college. In my freshman year, I noticed almost every girl paired yoga pants with UGG boots—a look I call the "campus cutie combo." I wanted to be a campus cutie, too! I swiped my credit card at the Providence Place Mall to purchase a $190 pair of beige UGGs and some leggings for another $50. I strutted around campus, showing off my brand-new boots in the snow, and I felt like the Sugar Honey Iced Tea.

When I came home to Bushwick during the holiday break, I was *immediately roasted.* My brothers and sisters teased me, and my friends on the block said, "OMG, look at Yanely wearing FUGGs. They're Freakin' UGGly!"

I would've roasted them back if I had thought those UGGs were cute. It would've been perfectly in line with my character to yell, "My UGGs are fire! I look *hot* with these on. Y'all just hating 'cause ya can't afford a pair."

Instead, I was literally shaking in my boots. That's when it hit me. I didn't find them cute at all. I still don't. UGGs look like teddy bears on your feet! My environment had brainwashed me, and it took swapping between two different cultures for me to realize I wasn't in complete control of my preferences. I was mindlessly copying what people around me were doing.

I was used to taking my feelings for granted or never checking for my feelings at all. I was like a sheep blindly following behind the flock without knowing why. *That's what the herd is doing, so I'm gonna do it too!* It's called herd mentality, or hive mentality.[10] When Beyoncé does something, the Bey hive follows. Yeah, that makes sense.

WHO WANTS MY MONEY?

I thought I wanted Jordans and UGGs so people would think I had money, but the surprising truth is that it wasn't about money.

When I break it down, I see that it was really about social status or being perceived as "cool." But, who determines what's cool? Advertisers, promoters, and marketers—that's who!

People around me were convinced that brands such as Jordan and UGG represented coolness and would boost their social status. For me, it was a huge game changer to realize this was directly related to marketing and advertising campaigns. Once I was aware of how ads were affecting me, I

---

10 James Surowiecki. *The Wisdom of Crowds: Why the Many Are Smarter Than the Few and How Collective Wisdom Shapes Business, Economics, Societies and Nations* (New York: Doubleday, 2004), 10.

became defensive. I approached each day as if I were heading into battle. This made me a soldier. Weapons and armor help soldiers defend themselves and survive. In this same way, consumers must build a defense against advertising and societal pressures if we want our dollars to survive!

We wake up and check our phones. *Boom*—a sponsored post wants our money. We brush our teeth and walk outside. *Boom*—a bus ad wants our money. We hit some traffic on our way to work. *Boom*—a radio ad wants our money. It's like playing an endless game of Whac-A-Mole...with a bunch of money-hungry moles! This is one major reason why you'll only get your money right when you strengthen your mindset first.

The easiest way to start is by asking, *Who wants my money?* Take a moment to consider why you spend money the way you do. These types of questions led me to study behavioral economics. When you dive in a little, you'll discover how advertising has evolved into psychological manipulation. Eventually, you'll want to know how to defend yourself as well.

In this chapter, I share key points I learned from studying behavioral economics and help you create a plan to get battle-ready.

YOU'RE NOT IN CONTROL

In the eighteenth century, economists believed humans always make informed choices that lead to their greatest benefit. The thing is, anyone who has ever regretted a decision knows this can't be the case. Herd mentality is far from rational.

According to modern economics research, people strive

to make a choice that's *good enough*, rather than the best possible choice. The research overwhelmingly shows how irrational humans are. It might hurt your ego to learn ways you're not being rational in everyday life. Try to read and learn without getting defensive. You won't always know what's compelling your brain to make not-so-smart money decisions. I hope that by the time you've reached the end of this book, you'll at least understand the need to check up on your impulses to spend before pulling out your wallet or phone.

This section is about my imaginary uncles and aunties in behavioral economics and behavioral science. Well, they're not imaginary—they're real people. I just imagine they're my uncles and aunties. You get it.

I'll start with Uncle Richie. My partner, Jamil, makes fun of me for calling economist Richard Thaler "Uncle Richie." But the man changed my life! I think about his work all the time. As a Nobel Peace Prize-winning economist, he's earned some respect on his name. He set up experiments that are basically like optical illusions, but with money. For example, he asked people, "If you're about to buy a clock for $25 but then learn that the same clock is available for $20 at another store ten minutes away, would you drive to the other location to save $5?" Most people said yes. Then he asked, "What if the clock were $500 and that store ten minutes away was selling it for $495?" Everyone was like, "No, no, no. I would not drive ten minutes for that. It's not worth the savings."[11]

Then, Uncle Richie came through with the facts. He pointed out that this is a completely irrational choice because in both scenarios, the outcome is exactly the same: you drive

---

11   Richard H. Thaler, *Misbehaving: The Making of Behavioral Economics* (New York: W. W. Norton & Company, 2015), 20.

ten minutes to save $5. When the participants realized he was right, Uncle Richie asked them once again if they'd drive the ten minutes to get the $495 clock, and they all said "no" again! Think about that for a second. We're such irrational creatures that even when we know our decisions aren't logical, we still make them the same way again.

In another study, Uncle Richie investigated people's feelings about what he calls "sunk costs." Let's say you're at an outdoor concert and it starts to rain. Would you stay and get completely soaked or would you leave? Well, your answer likely depends on how much you paid for the tickets! Participants in this study said if they paid about $40, they would leave the concert. However, if the tickets were about $400, they'd stay because they felt like they needed to get their "money's worth." Again, the financial outcome is the same either way. Choosing to stand in the rain won't get them their money back. But when things cost more, we tend to feel differently about them because money messes with our feelings. In this case, it feels like they wasted $400 versus only $40.[12]

But again, Uncle Richie comes through with the facts. The money you spent for the ticket has already been spent. It's gone and nothing you do will change that. Therefore, the dollar amount spent really doesn't matter. You should make the decision based on how you prefer to spend that time: standing in the rain at the concert, or being somewhere else where you're nice and dry.[13]

We're not always rational when it comes to money because our behavior is often a result of how we're feeling.

---

12   Thaler, *Misbehaving*, 66.

13   Thaler, *Misbehaving*, 64–72.

Feelings and emotions get in the way of our brain's ability to use logic to make decisions.

WHAT'S HAPPENING IN OUR BRAINS

Do you know our brains respond to popular brands the same way they do to gambling and cocaine? Yep! We know this because of Uncle Steve—Professor Steven Quartz from the California Institute of Technology. He's a neuroscientist who conducted a study in which people's brains were scanned by an MRI machine while they viewed images of popular items and brands. They looked at the coolest cars, clothes, shoes, and electronics of that specific time.

To understand the results of this study, you first need to know that active parts of your brain require more oxygen than passive parts where there's no activity. To provide this level of oxygen, your blood flows to the active parts of your brain. That's how Uncle Steve and his team were able to draw conclusions about people's brain activity based on MRI scans. They found out that the part of your brain that gets activated by looking at things you think are cool is the exact same part of your brain that gets activated when you win at gambling or snort cocaine. For my fellow nerds, this little part of the brain is the ventral striatum.

When I first learned this, I thought back to my desperation for Jordans in middle school and UGGs in college. I realized there was no need for me to feel ashamed about this. Uncle Steve's research proves my irrational spending was caused by normal, biological reactions to societal pressures. The bottom line is I was not in control of my own brain, and it's very likely you're not in control of yours either!

I don't know about you, but I don't want anything mess-ing with my brain and altering its activity the way drugs do. I want to be in full control of what I think and how I act. Today, if I walk past a window display and see a Gucci shirt or Fendi purse that catches my attention, I don't even trust my own brain! I do a triple take, asking myself whether I really find this thing appealing or if it's just my brain doing what it would do if I were addicted to drugs...or purses.

At the end of this chapter, I list a few other strategies that can help you put the research to good use. That way, you don't have to worry too much about all this mind manipulation stuff. But first, let me tell you about two final studies that can help you prepare for the future.

CHOOSING CHOCOLATE

Uncle Shlomo's full name is Shlomo Benartzi. He has a juicy TED Talk called "Saving for Tomorrow, Tomorrow," in which he shares an insightful study about how we view our future selves.[14]

At a conference, the audience was asked to predict whether they'd choose a banana or a chocolate as their snack during the following week's gathering. Seventy-four percent believed they'd choose a banana. But when it came down to actually making the decision seven days later, 70 percent ended up choosing chocolate.

This research shows that we think we're perfect in the future. *Future Me will do everything better than Current Me!*

I haven't had a chance yet to research ways to improve my credit score, but Future Me will have more free time to do it.

---

14   Shlomo Benartzi, "Save for Tomorrow, Tomorrow," filmed November 9, 2011, at
     TEDSalon NY2011, New York, NY, TED video, 17:29, https://www.ted.com/talks/
     shlomo_benartzi_saving_for_tomorrow_tomorrow.

I'm too busy to make a budget right now, but when I'm done with this class, Future Me will get to it.

I can't really invest for retirement because I'm tight on cash, but when I get a raise, Future Me will put part of that money aside for it.

We delay these important action steps without recognizing that Future Me and Current Me are the *exact same person.* If you're not prioritizing something today, chances are you're not going to magically act on it later. Change happens when you don't accept any more excuses from Current You and just start putting in the work. It's the only way to guarantee Future You won't end up choosing chocolate.

LITTLE BY LITTLE

We tend to be more reckless in the present when we know our future selves will have an opportunity to do better. I learned this from Auntie Wendy. Wendy De La Rosa is a behavioral scientist with a PhD in consumer behavior from Stanford University. She is also the co-founder of the Common Cents Lab, which is committed to helping low- to moderate-income people improve their financial wellness.

In a case study about the spending patterns of families receiving government benefits, Wendy and her team found that changing the environment creates behavioral changes. Each family received monthly funds in one big payment, or lump sum, but Auntie Wendy and her team used a mobile app as an intervention. Some families checked the app and saw their full monthly balance, while others logged in and saw the smaller weekly balance available instead. This small change "anchored them to a weekly spendable amount," and it led to big results!

Families who saw their benefits in one monthly lump sum usually ran out before the month was up. But when the money was viewed weekly instead, most families were able to make the funds last much longer. On average they were able to provide six additional meals per month! They weren't conditioned to seeing lump sum payments, so they managed the money little by little, visualizing smaller, more frequent payments.[15]

A similar study in Peru showed that families getting paid weekly were less likely to spend money at the start of the month on things like sweets, snacks, and booze. Better money management and more responsible use of money—that's a double win![16]

It makes sense when you think about it because getting a lump sum of money tends to create a false sense of abundance. You can easily find yourself spending more than you should because you have access to more cash than you normally do. A lot of people live like kings and queens for a few days per year when their income tax refund check hits or, in the case of college students, that student loan refund comes in. Teens looking at their first paycheck tend to feel like they just made two million bucks, even though it's usually more like two hundred bucks after taxes. If you've had a similar experience, you can probably relate!

---

15 "Using Mental Models to Manage Food Stamps Efficiently," Center for Advanced Hindsight, December 8, 2017, https://advanced-hindsight.com/case-study/managing-snap/.

16 Justin S. White and Sanjay Basu, "Does the Benefits Schedule of Cash Assistance Programs Affect the Purchase of Temptation Goods? Evidence from Peru," *Journal of Health Economics* 46 (March 2016), https://doi.org/10.1016/j.jhealeco.2016.01.005.

TURNING RESEARCH INTO ACTION

I know, I know—that was a lot of information! It's a lot to chew on at once. So, let's continue by focusing on ways to manage and spend your money more wisely. For extra credit, there are automated systems that require you to do only one thing up front and then let the system work out the rest. In this section, I share examples of strategies I've used in my own financial life, but don't feel that you must copy them exactly the way I present them. Pick and choose those that might work in your situation and are most likely to help you meet your specific money goals. You can also use my example as a starting point and later create a more unique system that works best for you!

PAY YOURSELF WEEKLY

This is for people who have at least one steady source of income. When money is consistently coming in, this system works like clockwork. Once I learned we're more likely to spend less when money flows in weekly rather than monthly, I opened a second checking account. I called the first checking account "Main Money," where my paychecks get direct-deposited twice a month. I named my second checking account "Fun Money." Here comes how to apply lessons from Auntie Wendy.

My goal was to set aside 20 percent of each paycheck for fun. Instead of sending myself 20 percent of my paycheck every two weeks, I split that amount into a weekly budget of 10 percent per check. I set up an automatic recurring transfer from Main Money into Fun Money every Friday. The amount was equal to 10 percent of my paycheck.

My rent, bills, and other necessities all get paid directly

from Main Money, and I rarely log into that account throughout the month. Remember that seeing a lump sum of money can invite a false sense of abundance, and we don't like her! I personally find it's best not to even look at that money because *it's not for me.* The debit card for Main Money is locked in my closet, and I never touch it because all my bills are on auto-pay. This makes it easy to know how much money I can spend on things besides monthly bills. It also made it easier to resist swiping my credit card every time that little voice in my head whispered, *Treat yo' self.*

To be clear, occasionally treating yourself is often a key part of your financial journey. Whenever we say "treat yo' self," we're actually talking about experiencing joy. The key is to also find joy in ways that involve little to no money. I spent plenty of weekend afternoons with my nephews doing low-budget art projects or reading with my boyfriend at the park. Just pack a lunch and bring a really good book, and you've got a cute, money-free date!

If you don't have a steady income right now, the best way to adapt this system for yourself is to figure out how much money you need to get by in a week. Once you know that amount, manually transfer it to your Fun Money account on the same day each week. Why would anyone do this manually? Because if there's a week when money is extra tight, you may not have the funds in your Main Money account. You might need to lean on a credit card until you book a few more gigs and bring in some extra cash. It might also be the case that you have a really amazing week or month when you bring in a lot of extra money from extra gigs. In that case, you should leave that money in your Main Money account or transfer it to a high yield savings account. The point is to just forget about it. Trust me, you'll be so glad you did when money's tight in a future week. Future You will thank you.

CHECK YOURSELF BEFORE YOU WRECK YOURSELF

We've established that Future You won't make better choices than those Current You is making. To deal with this, experts suggest entering into binding contracts that give Future You no choice but to accept that better money decisions were already made by Past You.

In 2014, I started my second job running an after-school program at a private education company. As the director, I was offered a 401(k) retirement investing plan as part of my benefits package. At that point, I was about six months into my debt-free journey and had probably read about a dozen personal finance books. (For a full list of my top recommended personal finance books, download your free guide at mindyourmoneybook.com.)

Reading up on financial topics, including behavioral economics, taught me to remain aware of the dangers of trusting Future Me to make all the right money choices on her own. When I signed up for the 401(k), I read through the fine print and noticed a checkbox that would automatically increase the amount of money I contributed to my retirement plan every year as long as I was still working for the company. I recognized this was exactly the type of binding contract Uncle Shlomo and so many others mentioned in their work. I had never checked a box that fast before in my life!

It's clear from all the research that automating annual increases to your retirement plan contributions is incredibly powerful, even if it's only going up 1 percent. Honestly, I never even noticed when the change happened, but it really added up in the long run. I knew the company wouldn't match more than ten percent of my salary, so I wrote in ten percent as the maximum contribution I would allow. That meant once I hit ten percent, there would be no more automatic increases.

My first year at the company, I was making $56,000 annually and my contribution was set to 6 percent of my salary. I put in a total of $3,360 that year, and my company matched it! In my second year, I got a raise and my new salary was $61,000. The automatic increase I had signed up for made my 401(k) contribution go up to 7 percent. So, by doing absolutely nothing in year two, my contribution rose to $4,270. Plus, I got that company match!

This is one of my proudest financial moves because Future Me didn't even have to make a choice at all! It was my way of forcing Future Me to choose the banana over chocolate. If this is a bit confusing to you now, don't worry. We talk more in Chapter 7 about 401(k) plans and investing.

LOVE YOUR STUFF

I'm not going to tell you to never spend your money. That's not realistic. But I will tell you to be certain that whatever you buy is actually valuable to you. I have my reasons for deciding that spending almost $200 on a pair of AirPods was worth it: I listen to a lot of podcasts and audiobooks, I record videos for YouTube and for clients, and I'm usually on the go. Spending $200 on a Gucci belt, however, does *not* make sense for me. When I was seventeen though, I would've probably bought both because I wasn't self-aware enough to discern between what was truly useful and what I had been brainwashed to want.

You can design a decision-making process of your own, or use an existing one like I did. My favorite comes from Tiffany Aliche, who is also known as "The Budgetnista." I've had the honor of speaking alongside Tiffany onstage and, let me tell you, she's the real deal. Her book *Get Good with Money* is a *New York Times* bestseller for a reason![17] Tiffany provides four questions to ask yourself before buying anything, particularly if you struggle to meet your financial goals:

1. *Do I need it?*
2. *Do I love it?*
3. *Do I like it?*
4. *Do I want it?*

Is it something you *actually* need and don't already have? If not, don't get it. Does that coat you just tried on make you feel like the heart-eyes emoji? If not, keep moving. It's okay to sometimes buy things you like and want even if you don't need or love them, but only do this once in a while. Otherwise you'll have less money for things that genuinely improve your quality of life and truly bring you joy.

Whatever your process, actually stick to it! Write down your process, and list some purchases for which you're most grateful. When you're tempted to buy something you don't need, refer to these questions and that list of purchases, too. This hack is especially helpful since money sparks emotions that completely distract the brain and cloud logic. A step-by-step process or framework for making purchases is, by nature, a logical exercise for your brain. Reminding yourself of what you're grateful for helps you recall that you're happy with so

---

17   Tiffany Aliche, *Get Good with Money: Ten Simple Steps to Becoming Financially Whole* (New York: Rodale Books, 2021).

many purchased items you already have at home. This might change your mind about shopping unnecessarily!

Many personal finance creators on social media post about "cost per use" or "cost per wear." I find this to be a helpful extra step when making spending choices. To calculate cost per use, just divide the cost of an item by the number of times you expect to use it. If the cost per use is very low, that tells you it's either a great deal or you need to double-check the quality of the item. You might picture yourself wearing a new pair of shorts all the time, but then the fabric doesn't hold up after a few washes and now your cost per wear is looking pretty different as the shorts sit in the donation bin. On the other hand, if the cost per use is too high, you may want to find an alternative or buy the item when it's discounted.

The bottom line is that having a decision-making process in place helps you self-monitor spending decisions for Current You *and* Future You. Having systems in place feels good because it creates a familiar routine. The more you practice, the more awareness you develop to discern when you're driven to spend based on emotion rather than reason. Each time you flex your decision-making muscles, it has a positive cascading effect on all areas of your finances. Truly understanding what matters to you—what you most value and enjoy—leads to better budgeting, signing up for the right bank accounts, and making savvy investment choices.

SWIM AGAINST THE CURRENT

For many people, the math behind money is the easy part. The social stuff—that's what's hard! It can feel like everybody wants to know why you don't have the latest iPhone, a new car, or your own place in a trendy neighborhood. This is why mindset is everything!

Social pressure is a constant, invisible force—ubiquitous and unforgiving. It has only one goal: to make you feel like you're not cool enough. Since our human brains crave connection, we tend to swim with the current, along with what's considered cool. It can feel unnatural for so many of us to try swimming against current trends. On top of that, money is an incredibly taboo subject! Those of us who find the courage to ignore social pressures and prioritize what's best for ourselves emotionally and financially might still be uncomfortable talking openly about our finances.

One way I've built up the confidence to dance to the beat of my own drum is by watching other people model financial independence. I purposefully seek out independent thinkers, and read about their ideas or watch their TED Talks, Talks at Google, or other online video and podcast interviews. I search for and read articles with headlines like "The World's Top 50 Thinkers of the Year." I've watched countless episodes of Tom Bilyeu's Impact Theory on YouTube for free, and they've added more value to my life than most of the content I've paid to watch!

This might seem to have little to do with personal finance, but it's one of the most important parts of managing your money! As humans, we care so much about fitting in that we fall prey to biases such as herd or hive mentality. We follow the crowd and do the popular thing, wear the trendy clothes, or buy the hyped-up meme stock.

The key is to think for yourself and draw your own conclusions about what you should do, regardless of what anyone else chooses. Hearing thoughts and ideas from people who swim against the current is extremely helpful in building up your own confidence and motivation to do so. Of course, there might be times when you make a choice that's in line with others, but all that matters is that you build the habit of focusing on the *why* behind your authentic choices.

In the age of social media, anyone with clout is an "influential thinker," but are they *independent* thinkers? Make sure you don't have a news feed full of influencers who fail to push your critical thinking. Every important decision in life requires your critical thinking ability, and this is especially important when it comes to your money. Everyone wants to take it from you, and it's your job to protect your financial assets.

If I had been able to swim against the current throughout college and the few years after graduation, I would've had significantly less debt. When girls at Brown were rockin' that campus cutie combo, I wish I'd had the courage to admit, "That's not for me! Plus, it isn't something I can afford right now." Rather than going into debt just to blend in with the crowd, I could've been brave enough to defy trends. I wish more young people today would ask themselves, *Do I really like those chunky Balenciagas, or do they look like somebody vomited on my feet?*

My wish is that you discover what matters most to you and never let other people's opinions sway your decisions. I want you to build the confidence I lacked in my teens and twenties so you never care about what other people think of you or your financial choices.

As humans, we can't help but compare ourselves to friends, family, classmates, or coworkers. However, the internet has expanded our reference group. We now hop on social media and compare ourselves to celebs and other public figures. When you fall into these traps, you have to be self-aware and quickly get yourself out! Check yourself and just do you. Future You will thank you for it.

A CLEAN SLATE

Shortly after starting my YouTube channel, I was invited back to Brown as the keynote speaker during Senior Week. After my presentation, a student came to me with saddened eyes. "I feel horrible," she said. "I've wasted so much money. My parents are sacrificing so much to pay for me to be here, and I've wasted thousands of dollars."

Smiling, I responded, "Maya Angelou once said, 'Do the best you can until you know better. Then when you know better, do better.' You shouldn't beat yourself up for mistakes you've made with money in the past. Now that you know better, you can do better. You sat through this whole workshop, so now you have the financial awareness you lacked before. All you can do now is move forward, stronger."

I'll always stand by those words of advice. If the event ended and she returned to her dorm room to order stuff she didn't need online, it might be concerning. But that clearly wasn't the case. She seemed struck by the presentation, and I can't imagine that after opening her eyes to the world of personal finance, she'd just go on with her life as usual...because now she understood the financial consequences.

In moments when I feel financial shame or guilt, I reflect on whether I had the knowledge, tools, and resources to do better. Most of the time I realize I didn't. Usually, I was doing my best with whatever resources and knowledge I had at the time. It's a waste of precious time to wallow in guilt about past money choices.

My first week as a classroom teacher, I was told that each

day should serve as a clean slate for my students. All the veteran teachers agreed that no matter how the children behaved—or misbehaved—the previous day, week, or month, a new day meant a fresh start! At first, it seemed impossible for me to apply this in my classroom because my mind was naturally trying to categorize kids into simplistic buckets such as "shy," "chatty," "well-behaved," or "naughty."

I quickly realized this way of thinking only made my job harder and less enjoyable. It robbed me of my joy and robbed the students of their natural curiosity. I wouldn't want people to evaluate me daily based on my past mistakes, so why should my students deserve that? Having a clean slate each day gives children the space to feel comfortable making mistakes, try again, and grow.

Here's the thing: this applies to adults, too! We need to be kind to ourselves, giving ourselves that same chance at a clean slate each morning. The only way to create that clean slate is to look in the opposite direction of the past. We have to focus on our financial present and future. That's why our aunties and uncles in behavioral economics never talk about Past Me. Only Current Me and Future Me can help me get my money right.

This is especially important if you're struggling with debt. Several studies show that roughly one in three Americans has regrets about their debt.[18] The top debt regret is borrowing money for shopping. I know a thing or two about that! Other debt regrets high on the list include taking out student loans and car loans. When someone borrows money from a bank

---

18   Myles Ma, "Americans' Big Regret of the Past Decade? Taking on Debt," *Policy Genius* (blog), December 18, 2019, https://www.policygenius.com/blog/new-decade-resolution-survey/; Jennifer McDermott, "Got Debt Regret?," Finder.com, last modified April 14, 2021, https://www.finder.com/americas-debt-regret.

for the first time, it's likely that as a financial newbie they don't fully understand how interest fees work. The terms and conditions may look and sound like a foreign language, but they apply anyway because they're trying to do the best they can with their available resources and knowledge.

Take time here to pause and forgive yourself for whatever money mistakes you've made in the past. Now that you have this book, you know better and can commit to doing better. If that feels intimidating, shift your focus instead to how incredibly empowering it feels to commit to your financial improvement!

Next up, we dive into the knowledge you need for twenty-first-century banking.

CHAPTER 3

Don't Bank with Mean Girls

IN TINA FEY'S 2004 ICONIC CULT CLASSIC FILM, *MEAN Girls*, a large high school is ruled by a small group of popular girls called the Plastics. In the United States, a large financial sector is ruled by a small group of popular banks that *issue* plastic. I'm convinced Tina wrote the script for *Mean Girls* to make a statement about the American banking system. Okay, obviously not. But the similarities are wild!

The movie's ringleader, Regina George, pretends to be nice to everyone, but behind their backs she's manipulative and self-absorbed. The only reason she's popular is because she's filthy rich. Well, big banks are manipulative, self-absorbed, and very, very rich. In the same way the Plastics have power and influence over everyone at their school, big banks have power and influence over our lives. They control and manage our bank accounts, credit cards, retirement investments, home mortgages, and all the laws surrounding those things! They gain and maintain power by donating massive amounts of money to politicians.

A website called OpenSecrets.org shares charts and graphs that give people a better understanding of how money is spent in politics. According to the site, big banks have lobbied heavily to reduce, or even reverse, regulations meant to protect customers and bring reform to Wall Street after the 2008 recession. Every year from 2009 through 2021, between $50 million and $67 million was spent on annual lobbying of commercial banks.[19] You can be sure the system is being run in a way that benefits the banks and not their customers.

Big banks have a reputation for using dirty tricks to maximize profits. A perfect example of this is my story of the first time I met with a banker. After my Sweet Sixteen, I had a stack of birthday cards filled with cash. I wanted to keep the money safe, so I asked Mami to take me to the bank. We didn't do any comparison shopping. We just walked to the bank that was closest to our home. Had I spent one minute researching, I would've discovered that community banks and credit unions just a few blocks further offered better rates for the same products and services. Most people do what Mami and I did. They go to a conveniently located bank or credit union and try to find a friendly face, or they go to the same exact bank or credit union *their* parents use without researching better alternatives.

Before I left for college, I realized I needed a bank that had ATMs near campus so I wouldn't be charged out-of-network fees. A major bank was conveniently located inside the campus bookstore. I called to schedule an appointment at a Brooklyn location, but it was incredibly inconvenient.

---

19 "Lobbying," OpenSecrets, accessed March 23, 2023, https://www.opensecrets.org/industries/lobbying.php?cycle=All&ind=f03.

Weekend hours were limited, and I was in school or at work during the week until 5:30 p.m. By that time, all the bank branches were closed. Mami was not going to skip church to go to the bank with me, so Sundays were out of the question.

It took a few weeks, but we finally got a Saturday afternoon appointment. There was one more problem: the banker didn't speak or understand Spanish. Mami didn't like that. I knew she wouldn't feel as comfortable during the appointment, but I did my best to carefully translate everything—as most children of immigrants do. By my tenth birthday, I had translated for Mami and Papi at banks, hospitals, welfare offices, parent-teacher conferences, and more. I had more experience than a United Nations translator!

We followed the banker into a small room and sat in front of his computer. I explained that I was going to college and needed to move my money into an account where I could easily withdraw it when needed. The banker recommended I open a student checking account. He said that as long as I was a student, most of the fees would be waived. That sounded good to me. I didn't ask a single question about the fees. The last thing on my mind was Future Me having to deal with fees once I was no longer a student.

The banker got to click-clackin' on his keyboard and opened *two* accounts: a checking account and a savings account. When he referenced more than one account, I interrupted him to ask why. "Umm, I'm only getting one account. Why do you keep saying 'accounts' as in more than one?" He told me they would be linked together for easy transfers between the two. This man really just decided for me that I was going to have two accounts! I never mentioned transferring money between accounts because I didn't need to do that.

I had only a small amount of money, which I was planning to use for my day-to-day expenses on campus. It wasn't realistic to expect I could save money in a savings account when I was paying for everything myself. That banker didn't listen to me. He was adamant that I open the savings account, assuring me how easy it would be to move money between the two accounts. He mentioned several times that I shouldn't worry because it was free for students.

Savings accounts are completely different from checking accounts! Both types of accounts have pros and cons, but each serves a different purpose. You can quickly and easily access your money in a checking account. That's because you can withdraw cash from your account at any ATM with the debit card that links to your checking account, or you can hand the card to a cashier to pay. Back in the day, people would request a checkbook so they could write checks to pay for things like rent, or gift money more securely for events such as weddings or birthdays. Nowadays, digital payment options have exploded and you rarely see anyone paying by paper check. Digital payment apps allow you to link your checking account to your phone or computer, making it faster and more convenient to send or receive money. Some examples include Zelle, Cash App, Venmo, Apple, Google, or Samsung Pay.

Savings accounts aren't as accessible as checking accounts. Although some banks offer ATM cards with access to cash in a savings account, it's not the norm. If you want to set aside money to grow for a short-term #moneygoal or unexpected expenses, a savings account is a great option. To get money out of a savings account, you typically need to transfer the money to a checking account or withdraw it in person at the bank. Here's the catch: there are limits on the number of withdrawals and transfers you can make within a certain period of time! This makes it inconvenient to use money in a savings account. As it should be! The whole point is for you to be saving. It's called a savings account. Hello!

That's how I knew I wasn't ready for a savings account yet. I had a small amount of money, and I needed access to all of it right away for necessities, such as textbooks, school supplies, and décor for my dorm room—but also things I wanted, like Starbucks and UGGs. I knew I would use cash or my debit card to pay for these everyday purchases.

The pushier a person is, the more annoyed and disinterested I become. As a seventeen-year-old, I was uncomfortable and confused. It wasn't necessarily a bad thing that the banker kept pressuring me to open a savings account—after all, savings accounts are good, right? They help us save money. Studies show that having a savings account at an early age is correlated with more money saved as a young adult.[20] In and of itself, pressuring me to open a savings account, which I didn't want, was not necessarily predatory. However, I later learned from someone working at the same bank that he was doing this because he had a minimum number of new savings accounts to open in order to meet the bank's quota.

Banks rely on collecting interest fees on mortgage loans, car loans, personal loans, business loans, and other types of loans. They finance these loans with the money that customers, like you and me, deposit into our savings accounts. That's right, banks lend *our savings deposits* to other people and turn a nice profit while offering us a tiny fraction in interest. In the summer of 2022, the national average interest rate

---

20 Laura Schlachtmeyer, "Here's Why Childhood Is an Important Time to Learn about Money," *Consumer Financial Protection Bureau* (blog), May 22, 2015, https://www.consumerfinance.gov/about-us/blog/heres-why-childhood-is-an-important-time-to-learn-about-money/.

banks offered in a savings account was 0.17 percent, while the average collected for a twenty-four-month personal loan was 10.16 percent.[21]

Don't freak out, though! Your money will be there when you need it because banks and credit unions are required to keep a certain amount of cash in their vaults. That cash is called "reserves," and it's required by the central bank of the United States—the Federal Reserve (a.k.a. the Fed). If banks prove to the Fed that they meet those requirements, they are permitted to lend your money out. Now you know why some banks offer you free money when you open a savings account with them for the first time, or why others pressure you to open a savings account even if you don't want one. Slick!

Most credit unions offer the same products and services as major banks, and they also lend our savings deposits to other people. But credit unions are different from banks in that they're nonprofit organizations owned and controlled by their members. At a bank, you're a customer. At a credit union, you're a member-owner. Any profits made by a credit union are returned to its members in the form of higher savings rates, lower rates on loans, and reduced fees.

Each credit union has a "field of membership," which means only people of a specific community or group may join. For example, many credit unions serve a particular geographic area, and only people who live, work, or attend school in that area may become members. Most credit unions allow members to invite family to join as well. Some large companies sponsor their own credit unions for employees to join.

---

21   Federal Deposit Insurance Corporation, "National Rates and Rate Caps," Bankers Resource Center, last modified September 19, 2022, https://www.fdic.gov/resources/bankers/national-rates/2022-09-19.html; "Consumer Credit—G.19," Board of Governors of the Federal Reserve, last modified February 7, 2023, https://www.federalreserve.gov/releases/g19/current/default.htm.

Religious groups, schools, labor unions, and homeowners' associations often offer membership access to credit unions for their communities. Historically, credit unions have had a reputation for better service compared to banks. Credit unions tend to have overwhelmingly positive ratings for their customer service, usually because they're smaller and more community oriented.

So why aren't credit unions more popular? Well, it's hard for credit unions to compete with big banks when it comes to the number of branches, access to ATMs, and technology like mobile banking. In 2022, credit unions held just over $2 trillion in assets, while banks held nearly $24 trillion.[22]

When Mami and I walked into the bank all those years ago, we expected a financial professional to look out for our best interests and offer solutions to our problems. Instead, we encountered someone pushing their own agenda and motivated by self-interest. Experiences like the one Mami and I had with the pushy banker add to the lack of trust unbanked communities have in the financial industry.

As of 2021, many people around the world were considered "unbanked," including 5.9 million households in the United States.[23] This means they use a cash-only system and do not have bank accounts. The term "underbanked" refers to people who have a bank account but still use alternative services for their financial needs, such as check cashing or

22 National Credit Union Administration, *Quarterly Credit Union Data Summary: 2022 Q2* (Alexandria, VA: National Credit Union Administration, 2022), 1, https://www.ncua.gov/files/publications/analysis/quarterly-data-summary-2022-Q2.pdf; "Assets and Liabilities of FDIC-Insured Commercial Banks and Savings Institutions: Q2 2022," Federal Reserve Bank of St. Louis, accessed March 5, 2023, https://fred.stlouisfed.org/release/tables?rid=482&eid=1217638&od=2022-04-01#.

23 Federal Deposit Insurance Corporation, "Despite COVID-19 Pandemic, Record 96% of U.S. Households Were Banked in 2021," press release no. PR-75-2022, October 25, 2022, https://www.fdic.gov/news/press-releases/2022/pr22075.html.

payday loans—alternatives that are costly. I remember my parents being charged ridiculous fees for basic, everyday transactions like cashing a paper check, sending money to a family member, requesting a money order, and more. For Mami, banking felt inaccessible due to the language barrier, her lack of knowledge of how banking works, and her discomfort in corporate environments.

In the case of Black Americans, there's no denying that many experience racism and discrimination. Past generations have shared lessons with their children and grandchildren about never trusting financial institutions—and for good reason. In the 1860s, when formerly enslaved Black Americans were freed, the government created social services to support these individuals with financial literacy and banking services. Congress created the Freedmen's Bureau—they actually put together the words "freed" and "men."

One initiative was creating America's first Black bank, Freedman's Savings Bank. Many formerly enslaved people fought in the Civil War and had received paychecks for their service. As they and many other newly freed Black folks deposited money into Freedman's Savings Bank, deposits reached $50 million in just a few years![24] However, bank officers were inexperienced, and they overspent on opening many branches, including a new headquarters in Washington, DC.[25]

They also allowed board member Henry Cooke to mismanage money by issuing risky loans, including one to his own company![26] When you're on the board of a bank, you

---

24 Jonathan Levy, *Freaks of Fortune: The Emerging World of Capitalism and Risk in America* (Cambridge, MA: Harvard University Press, 2012), 131.

25 Levy, *Freaks of Fortune*, 104–49.

26 Levy, *Freaks of Fortune*, 140–41.

shouldn't get a loan for your own business. That's a big no-no—come on!

The situation got worse, and in March 1874, famous abolitionist Frederick Douglass was hired as president of the bank. It was a chess move intended to strengthen the trust of the Black community. Trust was critical in preventing them from all running to the bank at the same time to withdraw their funds, which weren't there anymore! It was too late. The bank was already doomed when Douglass joined the team. But he didn't know that. Records show he invested more than $10,000 of his own money to demonstrate his belief in the bank's future success.[27]

Economic downturn led to many loans not being repaid—about $1.2 million, to be exact, according to records from 1874. (With inflation and interest, that would be equivalent to exponentially more today!) Just weeks after starting his work at the bank, Douglass suggested that Congress shut it down.[28] Records show Congress sent the Comptroller of the Currency to look over the bank's books and later the bank was shut down.[29] The life savings of one hundred thousand Black Americans got completely wiped, pushing them deeper into poverty for decades. It was a huge bubble of corruption. Henry Cooke never went to jail. No former bank officials went to jail.

The real tragedy is that the Black wealth was wiped away, and depositors were never made whole. They waited many

27 Levy, *Freaks of Fortune*, 144–45.

28 Levy, *Freaks of Fortune*, 145–46.

29 Reginald Washington, "The Freedman's Savings and Trust Company and African American Genealogical Research," *Prologue Magazine* 29, no. 2 (Summer 1997), https://www.archives.gov/publications/prologue/1997/summer/freedmans-savings-and-trust.html.

years to get back only about 60 percent of their money.[30] Just awful! If the government wasn't going to prosecute anyone, the least they could've done was find a way to get 100 percent of the funds back to depositors with a federal bailout!

It pains me that this money history is rarely taught in our school system. Students aren't taught the full context for why so many Black families don't trust financial institutions even in the present day. When we don't know the history—or choose not to believe the history—we brush it off and wonder "why Black folks are still complaining about this" generations later.

If you're scared that something like this could happen with your bank account today, don't be. The Banking Act of 1933 established insurance that protects our bank deposits. That's why you should always make sure your bank account is insured by the FDIC (Federal Deposit Insurance Corporation). FDIC deposit insurance is backed by the full faith and credit of the United States Government, so you can be sure it's legit. The same protection is available to credit union accounts through a 1970 law that created the NCUA (National Credit Union Administration).

Many geographic areas with little to no physical presence of financial institutions overlap with areas largely populated by Black families, even today. These areas are called "bank deserts," which tend to have lower median household incomes and lower average property values. Don't go thinking all these problems are now solved, that we've moved on from these types of issues, because banking is still inaccessible for many Americans. Many either don't have banks or

---

30   Levy, *Freaks of Fortune*, 146.

credit unions nearby or they're in rural parts of the country where a solid internet connection isn't accessible.

One 2021 analysis of financial institutions in Black-majority communities showed that Black borrowers and depositors face considerable challenges in accessing banking services.[31] This is why we rely on our laws to require that financial institutions discontinue discriminatory and predatory practices.

Most of us have access to a bank account, so we don't often think of others who don't. I encourage you to watch the documentary *Spent: Looking for Change*, which shows real people relying on pawn shops, check-cashing places, and payday loan centers to meet their basic financial needs. Not only is it inconvenient because these people go out of their way to put cash on prepaid cards or wait in line at a check-cashing place, but it's also expensive! The fees eat away at their hard-earned money.

As someone raised by unbanked parents, I thought I understood the struggle. Compared to some people in the documentary, though, my parents had it easy. Most services Mami and Papi needed were within walking distance of our home in Brooklyn. I never considered the experiences of my fellow Americans who live in rural areas and need to drive to the nearest loan center or check-cashing place. Add the cost of gas to all those ridiculous fees.

Some payday lenders charge up to 700 percent in interest

---

31   Kristen Broady, Mac McComas, and Amine Ouazad, "An Analysis of Financial Institutions in Black-Majority Communities: Black Borrowers and Depositors Face Considerable Challenges in Accessing Banking Services," Brookings, November 2, 2021, https://www.brookings.edu/research/an-analysis-of-financial-institutions-in-black-majority-communities-black-borrowers-and-depositors-face-considerable-challenges-in-accessing-banking-services/.

fees per loan![32] According to the Financial Health Network, unbanked and underbanked Americans spent $189 billion in fees and interest on financial products in 2018.[33] Even worse is that these practices are most prevalent in specific zip codes and neighborhoods. You can probably tell where this is going, and it's not cute.

If you or your family is unable to use traditional financial services, for whatever reason, this chapter might be more relevant once you're ready to establish an official account. For now, let's talk about the F word.

LET'S TALK ABOUT FEES

The Plastics required wearing pink on Wednesdays, sporting a ponytail only once a week, and never wearing a tank top two days in a row, or else you couldn't sit with them. Banks and credit unions have rules you need to follow if you want to bank with them. If you break the rules, you'll usually be charged a fee.

Not all banks and credit unions charge the same types of fees. Each institution gets to choose which fees they charge and don't charge. Federal law doesn't limit fee amounts, so banks need to follow state laws for guidance. There might be a maximum amount that financial institutions are allowed to charge per fee, but it depends on the state you live in. That's why it's so important to know the basics about fees and do

32 Megan Leonhardt, "This Map Shows the States Where Payday Loans Charge Nearly 700 Percent Interest," CNBC, last modified August 3, 2018, https://www.cnbc.com/2018/08/03/states-with-the-highest-payday-loan-rates.html.

33 Karen Graham and Elaine Golden, *Financially Underserved Market Size Study: 2019* (Chicago: Financial Health Network, 2019), 1, 5, https://s3.amazonaws.com/cfsi-innovation-files-2018/wp-content/uploads/2020/01/31170215/2019-Market-Size-Report.pdf.

some shopping around before you open any new accounts or decide to keep your old ones active.

You could be charged a $36 fee at one bank, while the credit union up the street charges $24 for that same type of fee, and an online bank might charge zero. This might sound insignificant to some, but when you're not a high-net-worth individual or a high-income earner, comparison shopping is everything! These amounts add up over time and can eat away at your ability to save or invest.

Letting bank fees get out of control and not paying them back can negatively affect your financial reputation. Banks and credit unions can deny your request to open a new account because of past accounts you had to close due to negative balances, outstanding fees owed, a history of overdraft charges, and more. The reporting agency most likely to keep track of any negative banking records is called ChexSystems. Banks and credit unions request information about your banking history from ChexSystems, including your risk score and your consumer disclosure report. This report keeps track of your public banking records like your name, Social Security number, past addresses, applications for bank accounts, unpaid banking fees, accounts closed involuntarily, and more. The only way to guarantee that no new financial accounts will be opened in your name without your authorization is to freeze your report on the ChexSystems website. Experts recommend you do this if you've been a victim of fraud or identity theft related to any of your bank accounts.

We know that most of the profit banks make comes from charging interest on loans, but they also collect a chunk of money from banking fees. A one-time $24 fee might not seem like a big deal, but multiply it across several million accounts, repeat it a few times per year, and that's a lot of profit for the banks! Banks lean on that stable influx of cash from fees particularly when interest rates are low because they're not making as much profit from charging higher interest on loans. As customers, we can and should refuse to bank anywhere that charges unnecessary fees, especially since fees and minimum opening deposits are significantly higher in communities of color.[34]

Here's a list of reasons you could get hit with banking fees. The next sections address more in depth each type of fee and how to avoid it.

Type of fee	What it means
Overdraft:	account goes below zero
Non-sufficient funds:	account doesn't have enough to cover scheduled payment or check
Account maintenance:	you get charged just for having an account
Minimum balance required:	account has too few dollars in it
ATM:	you used an ATM that's not operated by your bank or credit union
Excessive transactions:	you took money out too many times

OVERDRAFT FEES

One of the slimiest, slickest, and snakiest marketing schemes banks have gotten away with for far too long is overdraft fees. For decades, banks have hired entire marketing departments dedicated to maximizing profits, and overdraft fees have done just that! Bank regulators started collecting data about these fees in 2015, which was not that long ago. Before

---

34 Jacob Faber and Terri Friedline, *The Racialized Costs of Banking* (Washington, DC: New America, 2018), 11–17, https://s3.amazonaws.com/newamericadotorg/documents/The_Racialized_Costs_of_Banking_2018-06-20_205129.pdf.

that, banks got away with not reporting these fees—and they were going overboard with overdraft!

Service charges on deposit accounts, which include overdraft and NSF fees, have more than doubled while interest income has decreased during the past three decades. One report from 2016 shows that banks more than doubled these charges during the previous thirty years.[35] Banks with $1 billion or more in assets made more than $11 billion in profits from overdraft fees in 2019 alone![36] This shrunk to $8.82 billion in 2020, only because federal regulators encouraged banks to waive overdraft fees since most Americans were struggling due to the coronavirus pandemic.[37]

So, what exactly are overdraft fees, and why do I hate them so much? Overdraft happens when you try to make a purchase with your debit card but don't have enough money in your account to cover that transaction. You might think your debit card would just get declined, right? Not necessarily. A 2010 Federal Reserve rule says if customers "opt in" to overdraft fees, then banks can charge them for overdrawing their account. But why would anybody *opt in* to getting charged fees? That doesn't make sense. Well, when banks realized they needed to convince people to opt in, they stopped calling it an overdraft "fee" and renamed it overdraft "protection." Slimy. Slick. Snaky.

---

35 The Pew Charitable Trusts, "Consumers Need Protection from Excessive Overdraft Costs," issue brief, Pew, December 2016, https://www.pewtrusts.org/en/research-and-analysis/issue-briefs/2016/12/consumers-need-protection-from-excessive-overdraft-costs.

36 Peter Smith, Shezal Babar, and Rebecca Borné, *Overdraft Fees: Banks Must Stop Gouging Consumers during the COVID-19 Crisis* (Durham, NC: Center for Responsible Lending, 2020), 6, https://www.responsiblelending.org/sites/default/files/nodes/files/research-publication/crl-overdraft-covid19-jun2019.pdf.

37 Zach Fox and Ronamil Portes, "Overdraft Fees Jump 64% from COVID-19 Low," S&P Global, March 1, 2021, https://www.spglobal.com/marketintelligence/en/news-insights/latest-news-headlines/overdraft-fees-jump-64-from-covid-19-low-62873578.

In early 2022, headlines like "Major Banks Reduce or Eliminate Overdraft Fees!" went viral. A group of big banks announced cutting down overdraft fees, giving customers more leeway by letting them add money during a window of time before getting charged a fee, or getting rid of the fees completely. This is an awesome step toward a fairer banking system for everyday Americans, but big banks aren't making these changes as random acts of kindness. They're skittish about the new banks on the block taking their customers! The Plastics are scared to lose that sweet power, honey.

Many companies in the financial technology sector, known as "fintech," build entire brands around the idea that unfair and unnecessary fees are disgusting. The most popular fintech banking apps target teens and college students with a message that it's time to stop banking the old way. The Burn Book made its way around the block! We'll talk more about fintech toward the end of this chapter.

For now, here's a quick homework assignment: call up the customer service number for your checking account, and find out if you have overdraft "protection." If you do, you can choose to cancel it. You can also choose to shop around for a better bank or credit union to do business with and then add that old one to The Burn Book.

NON-SUFFICIENT FUNDS FEES

Just like overdraft fees, non-sufficient funds (NSF) fees are triggered when you don't have enough money in your bank account to cover a transaction. That's why a lot of people think these two fees are the same, but they're not! When you get charged an overdraft fee, the transaction was successful—the bank paid the money—and as a result your account balance dropped below zero. That's because the bank is lending you the money you don't have in your account. If you see an NSF fee on your bank statement, it means an automated transaction was rejected by your bank or credit union. That's usually because you didn't opt in for overdraft "protection."

Maybe you're thinking, *Aha! Overdraft protection does protect me from something!* Here's the thing: banks can't charge NSF fees for debit card transactions that get declined at the point of sale, when you try to make the purchase at the store or online. If there isn't enough money in your account and you opted out of overdraft protection, the transaction will just get declined.

NSF fees are charged only if you set up automatic payments or wrote a check. As long as you track your account balance and make sure you have enough money to cover upcoming automatic payments, you avoid NSF fees. At the time of this writing, the average NSF fee is $30 to $35 per declined transaction. Ouch!

If you've been charged an NSF fee more than once because you set up automatic bill payments, consider asking that company to change your payment date. Most people like to pay their bills on payday. You could also replace the debit card on file with a credit card that you can pay in full later. Doing this *before* the recurring bill date saves money and stress, while also buying you a bit of extra time to come up with the cash.

ACCOUNT MAINTENANCE FEES

Some banks and credit unions charge monthly fees just for keeping your money in their accounts. This is sometimes called a "service fee," and it ranges from $5 to $15 per month.

In most cases, this fee is waived if you meet certain requirements, such as setting up direct deposit or linking your checking account to a savings account the bank offers.

The easiest way to avoid this fee is to open accounts at banks or credit unions that offer free checking. It only takes a few minutes to search online for a list of checking and savings accounts that don't charge monthly fees. Trust me, there are countless no-fee options in today's world, so there's no reason this fee should be on your account statement.

MINIMUM ACCOUNT BALANCE FEE

Since banks make a profit on your money while you're not using it, it hurts their bottom line when you have a super small balance in your account. They want to make sure opening an account for you is worthwhile for them, so they encourage you to keep a certain amount in the account. For example, if your bank account has a $50 minimum balance requirement, you can't let your balance drop to $49.99 or less. If you do, you'll be charged a minimum balance fee, which averaged $5.44 for non-interest accounts and $16.19 for interest accounts as of 2022, according to an article from Bankrate.[38]

People who tend to have a low balance each month are obviously folks who cannot afford unnecessary fees. We should all have free checking accounts with no minimum balance requirements—and no fees for out-of-network ATM usage, which is coming up next.

---

38 Matthew Goldberg, "Checking Account Fees: What They Are and How to Avoid Them," Bankrate, September 27, 2022, https://www.bankrate.com/banking/checking/checking-account-fees/.

ATM FEES

Most people know what it's like to pay a few bucks to use an out-of-network ATM. That fee goes to the ATM operator, but then you might also be charged by your own bank! Avoid this fee by having a checking account that completely waives out-of-network fees, or one that reimburses you for ATM fees at the end of the month, usually up to a fixed amount.

EXCESSIVE TRANSACTIONS FEE

Prior to 2020, the Fed imposed a limit of six withdrawals each month per savings account. Even though they now allow unlimited withdrawals, most banks still set a limit of three to six withdrawals or transfers, depending on the type of savings account. Let's say the maximum number of withdrawals allowed in your savings account is five. The moment you make your sixth withdrawal—*boom*—you get charged an excessive transactions fee. This fee averages $5 to $10 each time.

Remember, the goal of having a savings account is to protect and grow your money by collecting interest. It's rare that someone would have more than six emergencies in a month, so most people don't have a problem with this fee. If you're tempted to keep transferring money from your savings to your checking account, consider keeping these accounts at two different banks or credit unions to force yourself to keep them separate.

This list is by no means exhaustive—there may always be hidden fees to look out for. Some banks, for example, still charge you for making transactions over the phone as opposed to online. Long story short, next time you plan to open a checking or savings account, ask about the above-listed services and fees. Make it your business to find out all the ways the financial institution plans to make money off of you!

For my banking, I prioritize accounts with unlimited ATM rebates, competitive interest rates, and no monthly service fees. It's important that my accounts match my preferences, but I had to learn how banking works before I was confident deciding what I want and don't want.

INTEREST AND EMERGENCY SAVINGS

The interest rate you collect in your savings account is called the Annual Percentage Yield (APY). The higher the APY, the more dollars you get. This is a very big deal when you're trying to build up an emergency fund in your savings account. Your emergency fund is basically a pile of money sitting in the bank that you'll withdraw only in the event of a serious emergency.

A hot topic is how much money to set aside in your emergency fund. Most experts say you need at least three months of necessary expenses, but it ultimately depends on a few factors. If you were to lose your main source of income suddenly and unexpectedly, would you be able to replace it quickly or would it take a while to secure a new source of income? The longer it would likely take, the more money you should save. Your emergency fund is meant to help cover unexpected emergencies like medical costs, car repairs, or job loss. Some people call it a rainy-day fund because it's there to protect you, just like an umbrella on a rainy day. Creating this fund is critical, particularly if you have debt, because it can prevent you from taking on more debt during emergency situations.

I personally feel comfortable with six months of living expenses in my savings account, but each individual needs to consider what is a realistic emergency fund goal given their level of income, job stability, and comfort (or discomfort) with risk. Once you have your emergency fund goal set, shop around for a savings account that will help you reach your goal sooner rather than later. This means you'll want little to no fees and high interest. Toward the end of this chapter is more info about comparison shopping for a savings account.

Big banks offer notoriously low rates on savings accounts. We're talking pennies per year on your $100 deposits. That pushy banker reassured me and Mami that having a savings account would help me grow my money. But when I did the math, it just didn't add up. That savings account paid 0.01 percent APY. For those of you who hated converting percentages in middle school, I've got you.

The word "percent" can be broken down to "per," which means *for every*, and "cent," which is Latin for *one hundred*. Percent means "for every $100." That 0.01-percent APY means you earn one penny of interest per year, per $100 dollars in your account.

So, if I deposit $100 into my savings account offering 0.01 percent interest and wait a year, it will grow by 0.01 percent, or one penny. Yep, you read that right. After a year, my balance would grow to $100.01. If I deposit $200 and wait a year, then my balance would grow to $200.02.

At that rate, it would take *thousands* of years to see a significant return. Nobody has that kind of time! Yet so many people open savings accounts that offer 0.01 percent APY. Big banks tend to offer these abysmally low rates, even though we already know they make exponentially more off of our money than we do. Despite this, big banks continue to serve the majority of American customers and hold the largest share of assets held by banking and savings institutions.

Many people feel disheartened by this information and think the system is designed for big banks to win no matter what wrongdoings they commit. It has been that way for many decades, but there's hope for change. Today, anyone can change their checking or savings account with just a few taps on their phone, so banks have more competition than ever before!

FINTECH CHALLENGER BANKS

Financial technology includes apps and software that help users with a long list of financial services. This includes payment processing, payroll and benefits, lending and borrowing, credit score monitoring, investing, insurance, digital banking, and more.

Let me be clear that fintech is amazing. The fact that anyone with a Wi-Fi connection can access financial products and services is revolutionary.

In the United States, fintech companies that focus on banking products and services are called neobanks or challenger banks. These are increasingly popular, especially with younger generations, but everyone should be aware of the pros and cons. Let's get the bad news out of the way first.

THE BAD NEWS

The majority of neobanks do not have FDIC insurance on their own, as traditional banks do. This is because most neobanks aren't legally considered banks since they're not chartered with federal or state regulators like big banks are.[39] When a bank is chartered, that means it must follow certain rules and regulations from the government. For example, all chartered banks must have FDIC insurance to protect their customers' deposits. FDIC protection typically covers up to $250,000 per account, per bank. This is a big deal because if a bank gets robbed, hacked, or completely fails, the government will return your money as soon as possible.

Neobanks can offer this only if they have a partnership with an already FDIC-insured institution or have a charter application approved, which isn't very common. As a result, not all neobanks have the full range of services traditional banks offer. They typically offer just a handful of simple products or services. These digital platforms require you to be very comfortable using technology and swiping or tapping to figure things out. Neobanks do not have physical locations for customers to visit. This means customer service is always done via live chat, chatbot, email, and sometimes phone. Many people enjoy exploring new technologies, but if you don't, neobanks might not be the right fit for you.

NEOBANKS AREN'T ALL BAD

The positive side of fewer regulations on neobanks is that it costs them less to get up and running. That means they can keep their products and services free or low-cost for users. As the newer, more tech-savvy companies on the block, neobanks can also speed up processes that take much longer with traditional banks. For example, if you apply for

---

39   Federal Deposit Insurance Corporation, "Banking with Apps," FDIC Consumer News, last modified May 3, 2022, https://www.fdic.gov/resources/consumers/consumer-news/2020-11.html.

a loan from a neobank, they skip the time-consuming loan application process and instead use algorithms to evaluate you. Their tech tools allow them to check your credit faster, speeding up the process of issuing you that loan.

The number one advantage of neobanks over traditional banks is convenience. While traditional banks are busy retrofitting old-school systems or procedures to a digital world, neobanks are digital natives! They've only ever existed digitally and therefore offer a much smoother user experience. Not only can a neobank handle your usual banking basics, but it can also predict activity in your accounts and use that data to prevent problems rather than charging you fees after the problems occur.

COMPARISON SHOPPING

Get in, loser! We're going comparison shopping! Just kidding—you're a winner in my book. For the highest APY offered in a savings account, you generally have to look at high-yield savings accounts from online-only banks or neobanks. While there are a handful of big banks with high-yield accounts, they tend to offer lower rates than the online-only banks and neobanks because they depend on that revenue to cover their overhead costs for physical locations.

Online-only banks and neobanks don't have to spend money on rent, bank tellers, and other costs associated with in-person bank branches or credit unions. That gives online-only banks and neobanks the flexibility to offer higher interest rates on savings. Big banks that refuse to adapt will eventually lose customers. If these banks want to retain existing customers or attract new customers, they'll have to innovate and compete with neobanks. In the meantime, the big banks are literally banking on you *not* comparison shopping, *not* reading the fine print, and *not* asking questions.

The fastest way to find a free, high-yield savings account is to search online. You can easily track the best rates and promotional packages on the latest blog posts from trusted sources like Investopedia, NerdWallet, Bankrate, and others. Don't ever pay for this information, because it's available online for free! Just search for "best high yield savings accounts" with the current month and year after it. Scroll past the ads to read all of the top personal finance blog posts. There might also be recommended videos you can watch, but I suggest reading the articles and blogs, even if you start with videos. Written articles get updated more frequently and remain relevant no matter how much or how often rates change.

Speaking of change, don't be afraid to change your bank account when you find an awesome new deal somewhere else. That's the whole point of comparison shopping from time to time. Data shows that only 4 percent of customers switched banks in 2018.[40] In general, people are unlikely to change banking institutions once they've used an account for years, and especially if they have direct deposit. It's inconvenient, and most people perceive it as a chore instead of as an upgrade to their financial life. I changed accounts at least five times before turning thirty, and I'm proud of Past Me for doing that! When you choose to switch, it sends a message to your old bank, credit union, or neobank that you hold them accountable. If they don't deliver, then you don't deposit!

Not sure if your bank, credit union, or neobank aligns

---

40 J. D. Power, "Ten Years After Great Recession, Innovation Overcomes Reputation as Bank Switching Hits Record Low, J.D. Power Finds," press release, April 25, 2019, https://www.jdpower.com/business/press-releases/2019-us-retail-banking-satisfaction-study.

with your values? Just hit up Dr. Google! Search the word "scandal" followed by your bank, credit union, or neobank's name, and be prepared to learn some shady things! Here are three examples:

1. The Consumer Financial Protection Bureau (CFPB) fines fintech $2.7 million over "faulty" savings algorithm.
2. A major bank pays $191 million in refunds and penalties for illegal surprise overdraft fees.
3. Another major bank agrees to pay $3 billion to resolve criminal and civil investigations into sales practices involving opening millions of accounts without customer authorization.[41]

Almost every bank, credit union, or neobank has been involved in some scandal, and it's your job to read about how bad it really was. It's one thing to be fined for bad data management—it's a whole other level to be fined for opening millions of fake accounts for people without their knowledge or consent!

If you have no idea what crimes your bank, credit union, or neobank has committed, it's probably time to find out. When I decided to change banks and level up my finances, I did some comparison shopping before committing to a new

---

41 Consumer Financial Protection Bureau, "CFPB Takes Action against Hello Digit for Lying to Consumers about Its Automated Savings Algorithm," press release, August 10, 2022, https://www.consumerfinance.gov/about-us/newsroom/cfpb-takes-action-against-hello-digit-for-lying-to-consumers-about-its-automated-savings-algorithm/; Consumer Financial Protection Bureau, "CFPB Orders Regions Bank to Pay $191 Million for Illegal Surprise Overdraft Fees," press release, September 28, 2022, https://www.consumerfinance.gov/about-us/newsroom/cfpb-orders-regions-bank-pay-191-million-for-illegal-surprise-overdraft-fees/; Department of Justice Office of Public Affairs, "Wells Fargo Agrees to Pay $3 Billion to Resolve Criminal and Civil Investigations into Sales Practices Involving the Opening of Millions of Accounts without Customer Authorization," press release no. 20-219, February 21, 2020, https://www.justice.gov/opa/pr/wells-fargo-agrees-pay-3-billion-resolve-criminal-and-civil-investigations-sales-practices.

account. I'm a visual person, and I like to write things down. So I made a simple chart: on one column I listed the options I was considering, and on the other I detailed the criteria that mattered most to me. One of the criteria was crimes or scandals I should be aware of. This might not matter as much to you, or maybe you just haven't considered it before.

If you feel this process might be helpful for you, make it your homework assignment tonight! If you can't find what you're looking for online, pick up the phone and call the bank, credit union, or neobank to ask them questions directly. Once you get a representative on the phone, you can say, "Hello, I have a list of questions I'd like to ask you because I'm considering opening an account." It can be easier to get someone on the phone instead of clicking around online for hours or getting frustrated when the chatbots don't understand your question.

Even if you have only a small amount of money to start with, comparison shopping matters. It's even more important in this case, because you'll need to prioritize accounts with low or no minimum balance required. Someone looking to move a larger amount of money might not care at all about minimum balance requirements. If you're saving up for a big purchase, you're likely more concerned about getting the highest APY you can, while keeping fees at or close to zero. It's important to know the criteria that matter most to *you* based on *your* specific financial situation and goals.

Having an easy-to-use app and website matters a lot to me, because I do all my banking on my phone or laptop. But I had to ignore that when I opened checking and savings accounts for Mami and Papi. They don't use mobile banking and prefer to speak to someone in person or get cash from the ATM. When comparison shopping with them, I made a completely different chart, which listed factors like minimum account balance requirements, ATM rebates, customer service via phone instead of bots, Spanish language resources available, and no monthly fees.

As your income increases and you're able to save more money, keep an eye on the APY offered at competing institutions, because that's where your money makes more money. Changing your bank, credit union, or neobank is a great way to ensure you're getting the most bang for your emergency savings bucks. I know it can be a bit of a pain to change accounts, update your direct deposit forms at work, and revise any auto-pay settings. But it's not so complicated or annoying that you should be stuck banking with Mean Girls or paying unnecessary fees just to avoid a small hassle.

Back when I was in college, I was broke and couldn't afford to travel. But after securing a full-time job and becoming debt-free, I traveled every chance I could. My partner, Jamil, and I watched the ball drop on New Year's Eve, right in the heart of Barcelona, Spain. And we visited Dubrovnik, Croatia, where many *Game of Thrones* scenes were filmed. Naturally, I decided to change banks so I would have no foreign transaction fees. Something like that would never have mattered to me before my lifestyle change! That's why we need to reevaluate our financial needs at least once a year, and we shouldn't be hesitant to change accounts when we find a banking institution that better meets our new financial needs.

The easiest way I've found to make the change is to transfer a little bit of money to the newly opened account and keep both accounts open for a short transition period. Direct deposit and any other new money will go into the new account pretty quickly. Then, you can gradually phase out usage of the old account by canceling automated payments and linking those to the new account. Once no bills are being paid out of that old account, you can close it by withdrawing all the money at once. Then, call the bank to confirm that you are indeed closing that account. It shouldn't take more than a few minutes, and it's well worth the time!

TOP TIP

When I got my first job after college, the amount of money in my checking account increased each time a new paycheck hit. I thought, *I'm rich!* That was a big mistake. You see, I wasn't taking my debt into account at all. The amount in your checking or savings account should not be your only financial concern. I was so fixated on the balance in my bank account, but meanwhile I had no clue about my financial net worth.

Financial net worth is the difference between what you own and what you owe. What you own includes cash, belongings, investments, and other assets that have positive financial value. What you owe includes any and all debts. When I was a teacher, I had no cash savings and owed $20,000 in debt. At that time, my financial net worth was negative.

Notice I use the term "financial net worth" instead of the more commonly used "net worth." I do this intentionally to avoid feeding toxic money mindsets. When someone equates their net worth with their self-worth, or worth as a human, it's extremely unhealthy. I encourage everyone to make this language and mindset shift! Financial net worth is simply a measure of your financial health. It is *not* a reflection or measure of your worth as a human being. My obsession with logging into my checking account was not healthy, and it was also completely misleading!

Even though it's called a checking account, don't get it twisted. You should not be checking it daily! If you find yourself logging in to your checking account constantly to see your balance and waiting for your next paycheck, like I used to do, then it's time to shift your focus toward calculating and tracking your financial net worth instead. This is especially important if you have substantial debt. I remember seeing my checking account balance increase and thinking I was moving in the right direction financially. Meanwhile, my credit card balance was simultaneously increasing!

If this sounds familiar or if it's something you want to avoid, then you need a clear system for tracking your monthly or quarterly financial progress. Using a simple financial net worth tracker can help you keep an eye on all your cash, investments, and debts in one place. Check up on your checking account from time to time, but don't let that stop you from seeing the bigger picture of your financial situation.

For an up-to-date list of all my favorite checking and savings accounts, fintech apps, and financial net worth trackers, download the free guide that pairs with this book at mindyourmoneybook.com. In the next chapter, we dig into credit, debt management, and how to get more from your credit score.

CHAPTER 4

From Struggle Bus to Syllabus

IMAGINE WALKING INTO A STORE WITH YOUR BEST friend. You're both shopping for a pair of shoes, and you happen to like the exact same pair! They're the same color, same brand, even the same size. #Twinning. It's time to pay for your purchases, and your friend is up first in line. At the checkout counter you hear, "Your total is $60." You're up next, so you put your shoes on the counter and get your cash ready. The salesclerk rings you up and says, "Your total is $130."

Wait, what? Your friend just bought the exact same pair for less than half of that price!

You advocate for yourself and say, "I'm sorry, why are my shoes $130 when my friend just paid $60 for the exact same pair?"

The salesclerk looks at you and smiles. "Well, your friend has excellent credit. You don't."

When you have excellent credit, you get the best deals on interest rates for borrowing money. Meanwhile with poor credit, you end up paying more for the exact same things. This doesn't happen with clothes and shoes at the store, but it does happen with the credit cards many people use to purchase those items! It also happens when borrowing money with a car loan, personal loan, or mortgage loan.

Let's say you and your cousin bought similar homes in the same community. You each saved up the same amount for a down payment and paid an equal amount in fees. You each need to borrow a $300,000 mortgage loan from the bank to pay the remaining balance and own your home. Here's where your credit score comes in. You get offered a 7 percent interest rate on your mortgage loan, while your cousin gets a 5.25 percent rate. At the end of the thirty-year mortgage loan term, you'll have paid more than $718,500 for your house while your cousin will have paid about $596,300 for theirs. That's a difference of roughly $122,000! As you can see, small percentage-point differences in interest rates make a big difference over time.

Lenders consider many questions about your financial situation before offering you a loan. They look at whether you have a j-o-b, and they analyze how much money you make. After all, how can someone pay back $300,000 if they make only $30,000 per year? That's why it can be difficult for people to access credit when they're unemployed, starting a new job, or being paid a low income. If you get approved, the interest rate on that loan is determined by the lender, but it's based on *your* credit score.

CREDIT SCORES IN AMERICA

As a kid, I always ran errands for Mami. A common errand was going to the bodega to pick up a few items we had run out of at home, like a loaf of bread, a dozen eggs, or a gallon of milk. More often than not, Mami had me tell the bodega clerk, Marcial, that we would pay for the items later when Papi got home from work. Even though I frequently didn't have money, I was always able to leave the bodega with bread, eggs, and milk. That's because Marcial knew my parents and felt comfortable extending them credit.

Marcial had a notebook where he jotted down who owed him for what, and he crossed the items off once we paid him. This was my experience in America in the early 2000s. Believe it or not, this has been happening since at least the 1700s. Even back then, merchants extended credit to customers and recorded the financial transactions in writing. They decided who did and didn't get credit, based on social relationships, just like Marcial.

In the early 1800s, a boom in global trade completely transformed how business was conducted in America. Individual merchants could no longer compete with factories that were mass-producing goods and sending them to big marketplaces. At those markets, merchants sold to customers with whom they had no relationship whatsoever. How could the merchants know if someone was financially trustworthy enough for credit? What if the customer ran off with the goods and never came back to pay for them? Economic sociologist Barbara Kiviat detailed this history in a revealing article titled "Credit Scoring in the United States," published in *Economic Sociology* in 2019:

> In the 1870s and 1880s, merchants started banding together through trade associations to share lists of delinquent and non-paying customers. Around the same time, independent businessmen launched the nation's first consumer credit

bureaus. These organizations collected information about individuals to sell to retailers, as well as to landlords, employers, and anyone else who might be interested. Agents asked around about individuals' debts, as well as other details that might reflect on moral character, such as drinking and gambling habits. The premise: third-party information could speak to a person's trustworthiness just like direct social connections could.[42]

As you can probably tell, this was not an objective process. All kinds of judgments about people were mixed into these official records. It led to early-1900s America being a hotbed of denying people access to credit based on racism, sexism, moral judgments, and other unfair or discriminatory reasons. Kiviat goes on to write:

> The US's shameful history of racial segregation and discrimination looms large in credit markets. Lenders, often aided by government, have systematically denied African Americans loans that might have helped start businesses or invest in property, and steered minorities to borrow under high interest rates or other unfavorable conditions. Early points-based systems for quantifying loan decisions codified the notion that blacks were less creditworthy by using race as a criterion and granting minorities fewer points. Into the early 1970s, lenders routinely used an applicant's race, both to allocate points—in one example, 7 for being white, 4 for being Hispanic, 0 for being black—and to flag applications for extra scrutiny.[43]

---

42 Barbara Kiviat, "Credit Scoring in the United States," *Economic Sociology* 21, no. 1 (November 2019): 33–34, https://d-nb.info/1217712542/34.

43 Kiviat, "Credit Scoring," 37.

Disgusting, I know. It wasn't until the Equal Credit Opportunity Act of 1974 that companies were banned from using race, sex, marital status, and other forms of discrimination to make lending decisions. This was a big deal because it meant any company that continued to allow the use of human judgment in lending decisions had better be prepared to defend themselves in court!

I'm sure you agree that these changes to the American credit system are improvements, but that doesn't mean the credit system is now perfect. Low-income communities and communities of color still have many grievances with the modern credit scoring system. For example, many of us lack access to "traditional" credit types like personal loans, mortgage loans, car loans, and credit cards. Those get classified as traditional credit types because they report your monthly payments to the three major credit bureaus: Equifax, Experian, and TransUnion.

So, you could be paying your bills for electric, gas, water, phone, internet, and other expenses every month but still have no credit score because those companies do not report your payments to the credit bureaus. Additionally, landlords, childcare centers, schools, layaway accounts, payday lenders, rent-to-own establishments, insurance companies, and secured credit cards do not typically report payments to the credit bureaus either. These are common expenses for many low-income individuals and people of color.

One of the most unfair parts of modern credit score calculations is that when you make your monthly payments on time and in full for a nontraditional account, it does not contribute to your credit score. However, if you miss a payment, pay too late, or fail to repay, then a negative remark is sent to the credit bureaus, and this hurts your credit score. Heads, you lose. Tails, you lose.

As individuals, we can't report our own payment history directly to the credit bureaus. There are third-party apps and services that offer to share additional information with the three credit bureaus on our behalf. Giving them access to nontraditional credit types in your name can help boost your credit score in just a few months. Examples of these services that are free include Experian Boost and UltraF-ICO. I like to call these "credit boosters." They offer a very valuable service because they analyze your bank account for consistent monthly payments and report those to the credit bureaus. Again, that's not something you can do yourself. We shouldn't need to rely on credit boosters, many of which cost money to activate.

The credit system is long overdue for further improvements. Instead of some services being labeled as "nontraditional" credit types, many could (and should) be included in our modern credit-scoring models. This would fairly boost the scores of many Americans who currently feel the credit system is not inclusive enough and doesn't accurately reflect their ability to make consistent monthly payments.

WHAT'S IN A CREDIT SCORE?

In my college courses, the professors each handed out a syllabus at the beginning of a semester. This was essentially a cheat sheet for how to get an A in the class. The syllabus listed out every assignment you needed to submit and every action you had to take to earn that A. Here's an example:

1. Mid-term and final exams: 35 percent of grade
2. Attendance: 30 percent of grade
3. Class participation: 15 percent of grade
4. Homework: 10 percent of grade
5. Pop quizzes: 10 percent of grade

In this example, the professor clearly weighs tests and attendance as most important, but it's cool that students know up front exactly what they need to do to get an A if they really want it. The same is true when it comes to your credit score! Most lenders looking at your loan applications pull up the most popular credit scoring model, which was created in 1989 by the Fair Isaac Corporation (FICO). This is everything that makes up your FICO score:

1. Payment history: 35 percent of score
2. Credit utilization: 30 percent of score
3. Age of credit: 15 percent of score
4. New credit: 10 percent of score
5. Credit mix: 10 percent of score

Instead of grading you on a scale from F to A, like professors do, FICO grades you on a scale from 300 to 850. Depending on the lender, you'll see different ranges and standards, but generally your FICO score will fall into one of the following categories:

FICO Score Ranges	Rating	Description
<580	Poor	Your score is well below the average score of US consumers and demonstrates to lenders that you are a risky borrower.
580–669	Fair	Your score is below the average score of US consumers, though many lenders will approve loans with this score.
670–739	Good	Your score is near or slightly above the average of US consumers and most lenders consider this a good score.
740–799	Very Good	Your score is above the average of US consumers and demonstrates to lenders that you are a very dependable borrower.
800+	Exceptional	Your score is well above the average score of US consumers and clearly demonstrates to lenders that you are an exceptional borrower.

Source: "What is a FICO® Score?," MyFICO.com, accessed March 5, 2023, https://www.myfico.com/credit-education/what-is-a-fico-score

Boom! Now you know how your FICO score is calculated. Remember the credit bureaus I mentioned—Equifax, Experian, and TransUnion? Well, they teamed up in 2006 to create a lesser-known credit score called VantageScore. You might see that score if you use fintech apps that help you monitor your credit. Still, make no mistake that most lenders in America check your FICO score, so that's the one to focus on. Now, let's dive deeper into the five factors of your FICO score and learn how you can hack your way to more points in each category.

FIVE FACTORS

Imagine if teachers or professors never told us how to get an A in their classes. Nobody would know what matters most, and students would just be guessing as to where they should put most of their energy. Some students might assume class participation is the most important part of the grade, while others would think attendance matters more. You probably already know what I and the other cool nerds would say... It's all about test scores!

Sounds a bit wild, but that's kind of how it is when it comes to credit. Lenders don't tell us we're being graded on how well we pay back loans when they offer them out to us or approve us for more. Since most of us were never taught about credit, debt repayment, or interest rates, we tend to learn by making mistakes. But don't worry—I've got you! Let's break down each of the five factors so you can get more from your FICO score.

1. PAYMENT HISTORY

Your payment history is the most important factor on the credit syllabus, comprising 35 percent of your total score. Paying your bills on time every single month is how you get all 35 points in this category. If you can't afford to pay the total amount you owe, at the very least you need to make the minimum payment by the due date for your payment to be considered on time. If the due date passes and you haven't paid your bill yet, up to 35 percent of your score takes a hit. Think of what happens to your GPA when you regularly submit your homework late.

Late payments don't get recorded on your credit report until they're at least thirty days past due, but the credit card company will hit you with a late payment fee immediately. If you ever submit a payment thirty days late or worse, that red flag stays on your credit report for up to seven years. That's almost a whole decade! Trust me—you don't want a late payment haunting you for that long. The later your payment is, the more it hurts your credit score. A payment that's one hundred days late pings your score more than a payment that's thirty days past due. If you owe a late payment, pay it off as soon as possible so it doesn't further damage your score.

If 100 percent of your payments for all bills, loans, and credit cards are made on time, your payment history is deemed "Excellent." When 99 percent of your payments are made on time, your ranking drops to "Good," and for 98 percent of on-time payments, you're at "Fair." Once 97 percent or less of your payments are timely, you drop to the worst ranking, which is "Very Poor." Everyone should try to avoid that, so let's talk about how.

Hack 1: Automate

Set up automatic minimum payments for every bill, loan, and credit card. You can do this from your phone or laptop. Just make sure you have enough money in your checking account ahead of the automatic payment dates. But as addressed in Chapter 2, you can separate bill money into your Main Money account. This will ensure the minimum payment is submitted on time even if you happen to forget. You won't have to remember to log in and make a payment, because it'll be automated. If you're hesitant about this step, I suggest automating your minimum payment (not your full balance) so you never mistakenly hurt your credit score. If your goal is to also avoid credit card interest fees, then automate the full balance to be paid on or before the due date noted on your credit card statement.

Hack 2: Ask for Forgiveness

If you've recently made a mistake and forgot to pay on time, pick up the phone and call your lender right away. Say something like, "As you can see in my records, I've always paid my bills on time. As a long-time customer, this was my first late payment. It was an honest mistake, so would you please waive that late fee for me?" Most of the time, this is allowed as a one-time courtesy. Just don't make it a habit! Credit card companies and other lenders want to keep you as a customer, because it's more costly for them to find a new customer than it is to forgive you. However, they'll be much less interested in helping you if you consistently miss payments.

2. CREDIT UTILIZATION

This one wrecked my credit score. Utilization makes up 30 percent of your score, and it applies only to credit cards and lines of credit. It measures how much of your total available credit limit you currently owe, because credit companies don't want you to max out your credit cards. Put simply, it compares the amount owed to the amount you're allowed to borrow. The less you owe, the higher your utilization score. I know this sounds counterintuitive. *Why would they give me a $1,000 credit limit if they don't want me to spend $1,000?*

You've probably heard people say, "Credit cards should be used for emergencies." Well, if you were to have an emergency and needed to rely on your credit card because the emergency costs more money than you have in the bank, then you'd need available credit. If your credit card is maxed out or approaching its limit, there's little to no room to charge emergency costs on that card. Your goal should be to always have lots of unused credit available. The less you spend on credit, the more points you get in the credit utilization category.

Utilization is super important, because it's worth 30 percent of your score. Think about it—that's almost one-third of your grade! You really want to pay attention to this one.

Credit Usage	Category
0–9%	Excellent
10–29%	Good
30–49%	Fair
50–69%	Poor
70% +	Very Poor

Source: "What's the Best Credit Utilization?" WalletHub, May 14, 2021, https://wallethub.com/answers/cc/best-credit-utilization-ratio-2140666075/

For utilization to be considered "Excellent," your credit card bill or monthly statement must show you've spent between 0 percent and 9 percent of your total credit limit. If you spend between 10 percent and 29 percent of what's available, you drop into the "Good" range and get fewer points. The "Good" range is still healthy, so it doesn't hurt your score too badly. However, if you spend between 30 percent and 49 percent, you drop to "Fair" and your credit utilization appears slightly unhealthy to lenders checking your credit. It's like getting a C in class. Spending between 50 percent and 69 percent drops your score to the "Poor" range, and borrowing more than 70 percent of your credit limit is even worse. More than 70 percent is considered "Very Poor," which is like getting an F. *Ouch!*

Hack 1: Divide by Ten, Then Spend

Whatever your total credit limit is, divide it by ten. This number is the maximum you should allow yourself to owe each month. Divide by ten, then spend! If you absolutely have to carry a higher balance, be careful not to bump above 29 percent, which will drop you to the "Fair" category. For example, if your credit card has a $1,500 credit limit, like mine did, dividing that total by ten gives you up to $150 to charge on your card each month.

Don't freak out! If you need to spend more than that, you can. Just log in to your account and pay down the balance right away to free up some available credit. The key in the above example is to prevent your credit card statement from showing a balance of more than $150 at any given time. Be familiar with the opening and closing dates of your statement cycle for each of your credit cards. If you always pay down your balance on a $1,500 card to $150 or less by the statement closing date, your utilization will remain excellent. Your credit limit may be higher or lower than the one cited here, so divide your credit limit by ten to gauge what you can spend.

Hack 2: Bump Up that Limit

Disclaimer: This hack is for you only if you've leveled up to the point at which you're using your credit cards wisely. If you can't stop yourself from shopping unnecessarily and charging items and activities on credit, come back to this hack once you've developed more financial discipline.

To get the best utilization rate, you need to use the smallest amount of total available credit. If your total available credit increases, the amount you owe takes up less space. But again, this works only if you have the discipline to not use the new credit made available to you. For example, let's say your credit card has a total credit limit of $3,000, and you currently owe $2,000. The credit bureaus see that you're spending two-thirds of your available credit—roughly 66 percent of the total. Now, if you call your credit card company and request an increase to your credit limit by $1,000, your new total credit limit is $4,000. If you keep your balance at $2,000 and don't charge more onto this card, your new utilization rate is down to 50 percent because you now owe $2,000 of the available $4,000. That's half of the available credit on that card.

In other words, two ways to boost your utilization rate are to make aggressive payments so you can decrease your balance or get an increase to your total available credit. Just don't get in the habit of increasing your credit limit while carrying debt every month. Remember the real goal! You want to have excellent credit because you have little to no debt, not because you hacked the system while still carrying a big ol' financial burden you can barely manage. That's *not* cute.

3. AGE OF CREDIT

Age of credit refers to the length of your credit history, measuring how long you've had access to credit. It comprises 15 percent of your total FICO score. Lenders want to know you've had some practice in the credit game. The main takeaway is that it's ideal to have an average of seven to nine years or more of credit established in your name. For your age of credit to be considered "Excellent," you need nine or more years on average between all your accounts, including the oldest and newest ones.

If your average age of credit is between seven and eight years, you make it to the "Good" range. An average of five to six years drops you down to the "Fair" range as you get less points in this category. An age of credit that's less than four years on average means you get little to no points in this category, so check out the hacks below to boost that age of credit.

Hack 1: Authorized User Status

Get in the game as soon as possible. If you wish you had started building credit earlier, consider talking to a trusted family member or friend who has a credit card they opened many years before you began building credit and kept it in good standing. The good standing part is critical because you want to piggyback off of good credit, not bad credit. Perhaps this trusted adult is willing to add you as an authorized user on their card. They'll need your name, address, date of birth, and Social Security number to add you to their account. This hack is a game changer!

A former coworker told me she added her infant son as an authorized user on her credit card, and the credit bureaus reported her one-year-old baby boy as having ten years of credit history. However, there's no real benefit to adding the baby that early. If she had waited to add him when he turned eighteen, it would have the same positive effect on his score, assuming she kept her card in good standing.

The tricky thing about length of credit history is that FICO doesn't add up all the years on all of your loans or cards. Instead, it takes an average of them. If you've had one credit card for ten years but no other loans, you have ten years of credit history. But the moment you open a new card or take out a different loan, they add those two lengths of time—ten years plus zero years—and divide the number by two. So now your length of credit history sinks to five years. That's a huge hit to this portion of your total score.

It's important to understand this so you can think strategically before opening any new accounts. Do you absolutely need that new credit card, or are you just trying to get the points they're flashing in front of you during a flight or a 20 percent discount off your purchase? The deals and discounts often sound appealing, but adding a new account to your credit lowers your age of credit as a result. Not cool.

4. NEW CREDIT

Imagine you borrow money from your best friend, and before you can pay them back you ask to borrow more money from a mutual acquaintance. You can't wait to hang out with everyone because that's when your acquaintance plans to give you the money they're lending. Instead, you get exposed! Your friends chat and figure out that you hit them both up for money. The mutual acquaintance now thinks you're not reliable enough to lend money to, because you still haven't repaid the money you owe your best friend. What a mess!

You don't want to establish a reputation as someone who desperately runs around asking everyone to lend you money. The same applies with bank loans and credit cards. You don't want to open too many lines of credit all at once. Every time you apply for a new loan or credit card, it affects the new-credit category, which comprises 10 percent of your FICO score. If you get a student loan, a new credit card, an auto loan, and a personal loan in the same month, it looks really bad and your FICO score dips by up to 10 percent.

To process your credit application, lenders need to perform a credit inquiry. This is also called a credit pull or credit check. Each hard inquiry temporarily lowers your credit score. To be in the "Excellent" range, you must have zero hard inquiries. One to two inquiries put you in the "Good" range, and three to four drop you down to "Fair." Five or more hard inquiries raise a red flag to lenders, wiping out your points in this category. While your score typically bounces back after about three months from the date of the hard inquiry, expect it to stay on your credit report for up to two years. Soft inquiries, on the other hand, are for informational purposes only and don't hurt your score at all because you're not applying for a loan. Soft inquiries happen when you check your own credit score, an existing lender checks your score, or a company checks your score to preapprove you for a promotional offer.

One annoying, yet critical, thing to know about applying for new credit is that even if you don't get approved for the loan or credit card, you still lose points in the new credit category because a hard inquiry is performed when processing your application. Each hard inquiry alerts the credit bureaus that you're trying to borrow money, and that's all it takes. Only apply for a loan or credit card if you have first done everything you can to boost your score before applying, researched your options to be certain it's the best deal you can get, and made sure you have no other choice but to borrow. It might sound extreme, but you can't go back in time or withdraw a submitted application for credit so be super diligent. Any time you choose to apply for credit, plan ahead and try to go six months with no hard inquiries before submitting your application.

Hack 1: Don't Do Too Much

Only apply to borrow money once or twice per year. Spacing out your applications six months apart ensures you don't have more than two hard inquiries annually. If you constantly have multiple applications in process for loans and credit cards, you're doing too much.

Hack 2: Get Preapproved

Don't apply if you're not fairly certain you'll be approved. That would be a complete waste, because if you don't get the loan or credit card, your score drops just for applying. Avoid this by getting preapproval, which means a soft inquiry will be conducted first. This lets you know what the odds are of your getting approved if you were to submit an official application, which triggers a hard inquiry. Always ask about getting preapproved before applying for loans or credit cards, because the worst that can happen is that a lender could tell you they don't offer preapproval, but at least you tried!

Hack 3: Authorized User Status (Again)

A little-known fact about adding someone as an authorized user is that no hard credit check or hard inquiry is required. The primary user on the account is vouching for the authorized user, who gets added automatically. If you want to add an account to your credit profile and increase your available credit limit, but want to avoid a hard inquiry, consider authorized user status as a creative alternative.

5. CREDIT MIX

The final 10 percent of your credit score is a measure of the different kinds of credit you have. This is called credit mix, or mix of credit. If you have a variety of credit types, lenders consider you a responsible member of the financial community who has practice managing money in different ways. It's a lot like when college admissions want students to show they're well-rounded. They look for applicants who excel in science and math, but also in extracurricular activities like sports or volunteering. Students who put all their time and effort into just one activity appear to be narrowly focused.

Having twenty-one or more accounts puts you in the "Excellent" range for credit mix. I know that sounds wild, but that number for total accounts includes closed as well as open accounts. If you pay off a loan in full, for example, the account gets closed but still counts toward the total number of accounts in your credit mix. Eleven to twenty total accounts are considered "Good," while five to ten accounts count as "Fair." A total of zero to four accounts keeps you stuck in the "Poor" category.

As you can see, the total number of accounts is important when it comes to credit mix, but so are the types of credit accounts you have. There are five main types of credit, and they can intersect with one another to make different combinations. The first two types of credit are revolving credit versus installment credit. Revolving credit allows you to reuse a certain amount of money after you spend it and pay it back. Credit cards are an example of revolving credit, because as soon as you pay off your credit card balance, it's available again for you to use on new purchases. This is the total opposite of installment credit, which does not become available again for use after it's paid off. Instead, you pay back the money in monthly installments until you reach a zero balance. Student loans and car loans are examples of installment credit. Opening multiple credit cards, while having no loans, isn't considered as healthy as having a credit card *and* a loan. The more types of credit you have, the better your credit mix.

The next two types of credit are secured credit versus unsecured credit. If you agree that, in the event you can't pay back the money you borrowed, you'll give something physical that has value to the lender, that physical thing is called collateral. You can use collateral to secure credit, or borrowed money. When you use collateral to secure credit, like a car to secure an auto loan or a house to secure a home mortgage loan, that's secured credit. The lender can take possession of the car or home if you default on the loan. Unsecured credit is the opposite. It means you borrow money without putting up any collateral to secure the credit. A classic example of this is a personal loan, which can be used to pay for general purchases that don't have a specific loan type associated with them. If you're looking to buy a car, you shouldn't take out a personal loan for that. You'll be able to get a lower rate with a car loan, or auto loan, instead. If you fail to pay back a loan, the lender can send your account to a collection agency, which adds a delinquency mark to your credit history. It can even go as far as their taking you to court and suing you to repay the debt, so don't play around when it comes to borrowing money!

Finally, there's service credit, which is when you pay a company consistently for a service it provides you, such as cell phone, electric, gas, water, and so on. Putting utility bills in your name is a great way to establish credit history, because it creates a record of consistent, on-time monthly payments that are reported to the three major credit bureaus.

Over time, you want to have various credit types that intersect with one another to create different combinations. For example, a student loan is unsecured installment credit, an auto loan is secured installment credit, a secured credit card is secured revolving credit, and a traditional credit card is unsecured revolving credit. I know what you're thinking: *Didn't we just go over the fact that the more applications for credit I submit, the lower my credit score gets?* Yes. Yes, we did. But the key is to open new types of credit as you progress through different life phases and might need to borrow money for your goals.

At age eighteen, you might get a credit card to establish your credit and help with your day-to-day expenses. Several months later, maybe you choose to apply for a student loan to cover the cost of trade school. By twenty-one, you consider taking out a car loan. In your thirties, perhaps you want to buy a house and will likely need to apply for a home mortgage loan.

Don't let the chart below overwhelm you. Slow and steady wins the race. That's the idea! It's not Pokémon—you don't gotta catch 'em all.

Type of Credit	Revolving	Installment	Service	Secured	Unsecured
Secured credit card	✓			✓	
Credit card	✓				✓
Personal line of credit	✓				✓
Home equity line of credit	✓			✓	
Auto loan		✓		✓	
Home mortgage loan		✓		✓	
Personal loan		✓			✓
Student loan		✓			✓
Cell phone or utility bill contract			✓		✓

Types of loans pulled from: "Consumer Assistance Topics: Loans," FDIC, last updated August 22, 2022, https://www.fdic.gov/resources/consumers/consumer-assistance-topics/loans.html

Hack 1: Out of Sight, Out of Mind

Put this category out of your mind. The best way to succeed with mix of credit is to let it happen organically. You simply apply for different kinds of credit as needs arise and whenever it's the appropriate time in your life to do so. This category is worth only 10 percent of your score, so you don't need to consider it as much as the other factors.

AVOID MAJOR CREDIT MISTAKES

First, never close your oldest credit card. The only exception is if the card comes with a very high annual fee and the company refuses to waive that fee. When you cancel an old account, it hurts your score in multiple ways, including the two biggest factors: payment history and age of credit. First, you lose all those years the card has been open and active, so they no longer count toward your average age of credit. Remember that scenario in which you had a ten-year-old card and a brand-new card, so your average age of credit was five years? If you cancel that ten-year-old card, your average age of credit drops to zero years. And if you think all the negative parts of your credit history related to that card will go away, well, that's false! All missed or late payments stay on your record for up to seven years, even for closed accounts. It's a lose-lose situation, because closing an old credit card account hurts your age of credit and doesn't even improve your payment history to make up for it.

Oh, and that's not all. The credit limit on the card you cancel gets cut from your total available credit. And you already know this hurts your credit utilization. Say you have two credit cards, each with a $10,000 limit. You owe $5,000 on one, and the other is paid in full. Of $20,000 in total credit available, you're utilizing $5,000, which is 25 percent. That puts you in the second-best range for the credit utilization category. But if you cancel the card that has no balance, you owe $5,000 out of a new total limit of just $10,000. This means you're using 50 percent of your available credit. This bumps you all the way to the second-worst range for credit utilization. Ouch!

As if that weren't bad enough, canceling a card hurts your credit mix as well, because you have one less account included in your total. Age of credit, credit utilization, and credit mix together comprise 55 percent of your FICO score, and when you cancel a credit card, all three of those categories take a hit. The older the credit card, the more it dings your score to cancel the card.

This happened to my sister without her even knowing! Her credit card company sent her a letter saying her card had been canceled due to "inactivity." She saw a big drop in her credit score, because she'd had that card for ten years, and it had more than $10,000 for the credit limit. She frantically texted me, "What do I do? Can I call them and ask them to open it back up?"

I responded, "Sorry, sis. Unfortunately, once they close the card, it's removed from your total credit available. If you open it back up, that will create a new hard inquiry just like if you were applying for another new card." Your oldest accounts should be kept open and active as long as possible. We'll talk about how to keep your credit card active without regularly spending money on it, but first here's another major credit mistake to avoid. Do not cosign a loan for someone, unless you're fully capable of paying all of their debt as if it were your own.

I made this mistake in my first year of teaching. One of my best childhood friends has a little sister who was having a tough time paying for college. I cosigned one of her loans, having no idea this meant I was ultimately 100 percent on the hook for all of her bills on this account. She was a great kid and promising student. She was on a pre-med track, and everyone in our community was rooting for her to graduate and go on to medical school. One semester in her second or third year, she got stuck because she ran out of money. Her outstanding balance owed for the previous semester hadn't been paid, so the financial aid office flagged her online account and she wasn't able to sign up for the next semester of classes. She needed a loan for the outstanding tuition.

Her mom, sister, and dad all tried to cosign, but none got approved. That's when my friend asked if I would be willing to cosign her little sister's student loan, and I agreed. At that point, I had a pretty decent credit score, but I hadn't started my debt repayment journey. I did have fixed, steady income from my full-time teaching job, and I had never missed a minimum payment on any of my credit cards. We sat at a table, she pulled up the Sallie Mae website, and I tried to read and understand it all. The language was very confusing—lots of legalese and terminology I could barely even pronounce. After clicking through each of the sections of the application, I was under the impression that, ultimately, my friend's sister would be responsible for the debt. I understood I was vouching for her application so she could get approved, like I might write a recommendation letter for her job application.

I was a recent college graduate, working as a classroom teacher, who actually read most of the fine print. However, I still didn't fully comprehend that I was taking on total responsibility for all the money she borrowed through this loan. But by signing that form, I agreed to pay all of her debt in the event she didn't pay it for any reason.

When I tell this story, plenty of people say, "You borrowed the money. You signed the paperwork. Did you expect you wouldn't have to pay it back? Come on, that's not how this works. You should've known what you were getting yourself into." I completely disagree. Given the lack of financial education in our country, it's not surprising that many people don't understand how the terms of a loan work. To those people who believe I "should've known better," understand that I'm the product of an environment and a school system that never once taught me the very details in the fine print that some people claim I somehow "should've known."

I didn't know how compound interest accrues or what amortization is. I didn't know how to explain defaulting, deferring, or delinquencies, and no, I couldn't tell the difference between a subsidized loan versus an unsubsidized loan. How credit works may as well have been a foreign language to me—and I'm not alone. None of the people in that room, where I cosigned, understood how the loan worked or its potential impact on our credit scores. We all had little to no understanding, but we did have credit cards and student loans! We should not be completely off the hook for our debts—some level of individual responsibility and accountability is needed—but higher levels of systemic barriers are at play that equally need to be addressed.

My friend's little sister did not graduate on time. She was missing some required credits but didn't have enough money to keep enrolling in classes. She considered pivoting into education or social work. She eventually graduated into an economic recession and had a very hard time finding a job. She worked at Best Buy to make ends meet until she could figure out her next steps. That's when Sallie Mae began sending her student loan bills to my apartment. She had borrowed $13,000, which I cosigned for, and that original loan amount had accrued enough interest to make the new total balance $17,000.

Wait, why is this bill coming here in my name. What's going on? I read article after article, horror story after horror story, and watched video after video. Then, I realized what was happening. I was frustrated with the situation. I was overwhelmed by the debt. I was angry with myself. I was fully responsible for these monthly payments, because I cosigned for that loan all those years ago. I wish I had understood that cosigning was the equivalent of co-owning.

The student loan bill stated that if I missed a payment, my credit score would decrease dramatically. I knew my credit score wasn't the best, because our landlord checked my credit before my roommates and I moved into our shared apartment. I called my friend's little sister and said, "Hey, so I got a letter about a $235 payment due on the third of the month. Are you going to make that payment?"

Her response was exactly what I had dreaded: "Oh, I can't afford to pay that right now." Cosigning her loan would ultimately damage my financial reputation unless I stepped in and took responsibility for the payments. So, I linked my checking account to her student loan account that same day and made payments whenever she couldn't manage. Then, I got serious about finding a solution.

Through countless hours of research, I learned that some lenders allow the primary borrower to request a cosigner release. This involves paperwork or an online application that removes the cosigner from the loan and places the primary borrower as the only borrower on the loan. I picked up the phone and called Sallie Mae to ask if they offered this option and was so happy to learn they did. I explained this to my friend's little sister and thankfully she agreed to apply. However, Sallie Mae had a list of requirements that we didn't meet at the time. To release me as cosigner, the minimum payment had to be submitted on time every month for twelve months. I thought, *Okay, we can do that!*

Next, both she and I needed to pass a credit check, which means we needed good credit scores. My credit score was fair, and hers was very poor. I thought, *Okay, we can learn how to improve our credit scores, too.* You've heard the phrase, "where there's a will there's a way," right? I had the will, and I was determined to find the way.

During the year of making on-time monthly payments in an attempt to be released as her cosigner, I also learned about debt consolidation, which is covered in Chapter 5. We managed to increase her credit score to above 600 by using many of the hacks in my credit syllabus. Before we reached twelve monthly payments, she was approved for a debt consolidation loan. She was then able to make one low monthly payment for all of her student loans. The following month, my credit score jumped by nearly 100 points.

Existing lending and borrowing systems need improvement and, in particular, better regulations to protect consumers. Where there's not enough regulation, there should be an abundance of education. Sadly, that's not the case when it comes to credit and financial education in America. I was bamboozled by credit card companies at the age of eighteen. It took me years to get out of credit card debt. I won't let that happen to me again, but what about all the college students after me?

Thankfully tighter regulations on credit card companies now completely ban them from encouraging college students to apply for credit cards in exchange for free swag. That should've never been legal! However, anger, frustration, and shame don't create positive change. We need to stop shaming people for what they don't know and instead demand financial education to improve what they do know. We also need to demand better regulation to prevent financial institutions from getting away with using predatory lending practices.

NOTHING LASTS FOREVER

Bad credit can be a vicious cycle. The worse your credit, the more challenging it is to improve, since it can be nearly impossible to get approved for any new loans. The good news is there are laws mandating negative information eventually be erased from credit reports. Even though credit bureaus accumulate all the data and include it in your credit score calculation, after a certain number of years, some data must be wiped so consumers at least have a chance to make a comeback.

The worst types of infractions, such as a home foreclosure, take longer to disappear than something like a missed credit card payment. This chart outlines negative behaviors according to how long they stay on your credit report: two years or less, up to seven years, up to ten years, or indefinitely.

How Long Will Negative Items Remain on Your Credit?

Credit inquiries	2 years or less
Late payments	7 years or less
Collections	
Judgments	
Settlements	
Foreclosures	
Repossessions	
Released tax liens	
Charged offs	
Chapter 7	10 years or less
Bankruptcy	
Chapter 10	
California state tax liens	
Federal student loans in collections	Indefinitely
Federal tax liens	

Source: Fair Credit Reporting Act, 15 U.S.C. § 1681 (1970), https://www.ftc.gov/system/files/ftc_gov/pdf/545A-FCRA-08-2022-508.pdf

The "Indefinitely" category is scary. That stuff might never get wiped from your credit report, so you really don't want to make mistakes there. And surprise, surprise—federal student loans and federal tax liens are the culprits! If you're in over your head with credit cards or personal loans, you can always file for bankruptcy. It's not ideal because it takes seven to ten years to recover from a bankruptcy, but it's a viable option.

However, bankruptcy does not wipe away outstanding student loan debt or federal taxes owed, except in extremely rare circumstances called "undue hardship." It's not likely a court would agree to eliminate student loan debt as a result of undue hardship because lenders generally recommend income-driven repayment plans or loan deferment. Millennials and Gen Z experienced the start of the student loan debt crisis in America, but all future college students need to learn how these loans affect their credit standing, regardless of what generation they're in. We talk more in Chapter 5 about repaying student loans, but first, let's go over something everyone must know: how to check your credit score.

KNOW YOUR FICO SCORE

Many apps and websites charge a one-time or monthly fee for you to access your credit score. Do not—I repeat, *do not*—pay to view your credit score. There are many ways you can access your score and other information about your credit profile—for free! Before we go through your options, know that absolutely no harm comes to your FICO score when you check it yourself. Checking your own credit score does not create a hard inquiry, because it's not an application for a new account. You can check your credit score anytime you want, and it won't lower your score. Did I mention that it's free ninety-nine?

The most reliable source of information regarding your FICO score is...FICO! Yes, FICO has an official consumer division—it's called myFICO. Anyone can create an account with myFICO and have their FICO score in five minutes or less. It's amazing, I know! There's just one itty-bitty problem: most people have never heard of the free option. On the myFICO site, it's easy to find premium subscription plans that cost anywhere from $19.95 to $39.95 per month for access to your FICO score, monthly updates, score and credit monitoring, identity theft insurance, and credit reports from all three credit bureaus. Meanwhile, all this stuff is available for free on another site or is completely unnecessary.

Let's start with getting your FICO score for free. Do a web search for the phrase "myFICO free plan." Scroll past any ads and make sure to only click a link that takes you to the myFICO website. Once you find the free option, select the word "free" and confirm that it states "no credit card required." Read through the terms, and make sure you're comfortable with those. Also be sure you're comfortable sharing your email address with myFICO. If so, start the plan by creating your free myFICO account by choosing a username and secure password. You'll need to verify your identity right away, and then you just log in with your new username and password to immediately see your FICO score on the screen.

If you don't want to share your email and all of your business with myFICO (even though they probably already have it) or disagree with the terms of opening the free account, you have other options. Check to see if you have an existing credit card or bank account that offers free access to your credit score through its website portal or by downloading their app. Most of my credit card providers allow me to see my FICO score in their apps, where I usually view my credit card statements and pay bills, so I'm lucky. I prefer using myFICO because most platforms tend to share your VantageScore with you instead of your FICO score.

CREDIT SCORE VERSUS CREDIT REPORT

Checking your credit score is only one part of knowing how healthy your credit is. You also need to check your credit report. Think of your credit report as your financial transcript, while your credit score is more like your financial GPA. All the information the credit bureaus collect gets recorded on your credit report.

Since there are three main credit bureaus, you should check all three of your credit reports. They generally have the same information about you, such as your full name, addresses where you've lived, your Social Security number, open and closed credit accounts with payment history and credit limits for each, any public records on file (bankruptcies, foreclosures, tax liens), and a list of any hard inquiries in the past two years. Sometimes one credit bureau might be missing information another bureau has. This could lead to your credit reports looking slightly different and can even result in credit scores that are a few points apart. That's another reason I prefer to get my credit score directly from myFICO.

With the free myFICO account, you get access to your Equifax credit report. If you want all three credit reports, including the ones from Experian and TransUnion, you need to visit annualcreditreport.com. This site is the only online source authorized by federal law, so it's legit. The law requires that everyone have access to a free copy of all three credit reports at least once per year. The process can be a bit confusing, because you need to go through a few steps over and over again three times, once for each credit bureau's website. You even have the option to download and print your credit reports for your records.

You can check back again in a year to see if everything on your credit reports is still accurate and up to date. If there are any errors or discrepancies, call the credit bureaus directly— check their websites for contact information. If you want access to monthly updates, score and credit monitoring, or identity theft insurance, you'll need to pay for that. Many people feel it's worth paying monthly fees for monitoring, protection, and updates since it provides them peace of mind.

Scammers are increasingly tech-savvy. They might get access to someone's private data online and then pretend to be that person by creating new accounts in their name. Then, they go shopping with the credit cards or loan money but have zero intention of paying for any of it. This type of identity theft and credit fraud increased after the pandemic because more people were shopping online and entering personal information on many different websites.[44] The best way to eliminate the fear that someone might steal your identity and ruin your credit is to freeze it.

FREEZE YOUR CREDIT

The purpose of paying for monthly updates, credit score monitoring, and identity theft insurance is to keep a close

---

44   Federal Trade Commission, "New Data Shows FTC Received 2.8 Million Fraud Reports from Consumers in 2021," press release, February 22, 2022, https://www.ftc.gov/news-events/news/ press-releases/2022/02/new-data-shows-ftc-received-28-million-fraud-reports-consumers-2021-0.

eye on your credit profile and sleep better at night. You want to make sure nobody applies for credit accounts in your name, and if anyone does, you want to ensure they get caught right away. Well, you can do all of that by freezing your credit reports for free. Placing a freeze on your credit report blocks access to that credit report, protecting you against scammers who may try to open fake accounts in your name.

Remember that, to apply for a new account, a hard inquiry is required. Lenders cannot legally check your credit score without your consent. That's right—nobody can access your credit report and credit score without your permission. Freezing your credit means the next time anyone, including you, tries to open a new account with your name, Social Security number, and date of birth, the system will not allow it. The hard inquiry can't go through until you lift the freeze on your credit.

How does freezing and unfreezing your credit work? I froze my credit in 2018. I went through the process three times, once for each credit bureau. I wish you only had to do it one time, because it takes a little longer than five minutes, but it's worth it! I never have to pay for credit protection, because I know there's no way new accounts can be created unless I unfreeze my credit.

When I froze my credit, I chose a very secure PIN for each credit bureau and stored them in a safe place where I could access them later when needed. Depending on your account details, you may need to create one PIN, or several. Either way, make sure you store these details securely. About a year after placing the freeze, Jamil and I applied to rent a new apartment, and the landlord asked to check our credit scores. I logged in to the website for Equifax that afternoon and, using my PIN, lifted the freeze for the following two weeks.

I did the same for the other two credit bureaus. What's cool is I didn't have to remember to freeze the reports back up again. The two-week term is a temporary time to unfreeze the reports, which lock back up automatically.

If you're going to apply for credit often, it can be annoying to keep unfreezing your credit reports. That's a red flag, though! Why are you planning to apply for so many new accounts? You know what that'll do to your FICO score. If you're shopping around for mortgage loan rates for a month or so, just lift the freeze for a month instead of two weeks.

To freeze your credit reports, visit each website for all three credit bureaus and follow the steps to place a freeze on those reports. Freezing your credit or your child's credit is completely free, so don't let anyone convince you otherwise. It's also free to lift the freeze for any period of time, and none of this negatively impacts your credit score! It's more common than you might think for children to be victims of identity theft, so parents might consider freezing their child's credit until they need to apply for their first credit type. That's typically a car loan or their very first credit card.

CHOOSE A CARD THAT'S RIGHT FOR YOU

The easiest way to establish credit at any age is to get a credit card. Once you're in the credit game, you can slowly improve your score and eventually negotiate for lower interest rates as you climb up the credit ladder. Remember, the higher your credit score, the lower the interest rates for which you qualify. Different camps of people use different frameworks to decide what card is best for them. It makes sense that everyone chooses differently, because people have different preferences, income levels, credit histories, and spending patterns. Everyone comes at this with unique goals and a unique perspective. The advice that follows is organized by which rung of the credit ladder you're currently standing on.

STUDENT NEW TO CREDIT

It's relatively easy to get a student credit card—not as easy as when I was a student, but still easy using online application processes. You'll be asked to enter your personal identification information like your name, date of birth, address, phone number, and more. When asked to submit your monthly income, many students get stumped if they don't have much money coming in. You're not allowed to list any money that is borrowed exclusively for education expenses. That means student loans do not count as income on a credit card application, but a part-time job, grants, scholarships, and allowance do!

Never enter false information on a credit card application, no matter how desperate you are to get approved. It's against federal law, so you could end up in deep trouble. If your income is too low to qualify for a student credit card, consider the authorized user route with a trusted family member.

Unlike traditional cards, which are designed for general adult users, student cards are designed with college students in mind. The typical student credit card is unsecured, meaning no deposit is needed to secure that credit. As a student, you have little to no credit history, so banks take a pretty big risk lending to you without access to data about your past borrowing behaviors. To make up for that risk, banks charge higher interest rates for student cards than for traditional credit cards.

That's annoying, because students are usually broke while

in school and that makes them more likely to carry a balance from one month to the next. But if you use a student card responsibly, it helps build credit and, in many cases, can lead to cool rewards and bonus perks. Student cards tend to have lower credit limits, limited rewards, and special benefits like bonus points for paying on time, or discounts like waiving annual fees and forgiving your first late payment. Student credit cards may earn cash back in certain spending categories or rotating categories, but they're not likely to offer generous rewards like sign-up bonuses in the form of travel points or bonus miles, and access to airport lounges.

A lower credit limit and higher interest rate, on average 3 percent higher than traditional cards, is a bad combination. However, unlike with traditional card applications you don't have to worry too much about being rejected. Most college students are automatically approved for student credit cards. Since getting rejected for a card leaves a hard inquiry on your credit report, it's good that you don't need to stress about this. The hard inquiry is worth it if you get approved and get to start climbing up that credit ladder.

Knowing you don't need a security deposit for most student cards is another sigh of relief, because students need money for things like textbooks. Banks realize you might not have a lot of money now but that you'll be good for it once you're working full-time, so they want to keep you as a customer. After a few months you can call and ask for a lower interest rate or a higher credit limit if you choose.

You benefit the bank even if you rarely use your card, because down the line when you need a home mortgage, you're likely to apply at the same bank that issued your credit card since that bank's logo has literally been in your back pocket for the last decade or so. The bank views you as a longtime customer, so see the value in that and use it as leverage to negotiate better rates and terms with your credit card company over time.

NEW TO CREDIT BUT NOT IN SCHOOL

Say you graduate high school and go directly into the workforce. You can't get a student card, and you don't have any credit history. It's tough to get approved for a traditional credit card in that case. The best approach is to save $100 to $200 from your first few paychecks to apply for a secured credit card. As you know, this requires you to agree that if you can't pay your credit card bills, the bank can keep that collateral (a.k.a. security deposit) you used to secure the credit. This is a shortcut to getting into the credit game. Use the card to buy things you need, and always pay it back in full and on time every month.

This should be easier to do with a lower-limit secured card versus thousands of dollars on a traditional credit card. View it as a good way to practice before using traditional credit cards. After a year or so, call the bank and say something like this: "Hello. I've been using this secured credit card for a year, and it's been helpful in establishing credit. I'm now ready to get my $200 deposit back and upgrade this account to an unsecured credit card." If they're not willing to upgrade you, consider asking if they can offer you an unsecured credit card that comes with no annual fee. It's better to increase your access to credit than to cancel that card and be back at the starting line with no accounts.

ESTABLISHED CREDIT HISTORY BUT WANT A BETTER FIT

There are so many cards out there, and they all offer different incentives—it's endless. Don't let it overwhelm you. The best way to navigate this is to search for a card based on your current goals or spending habits. If a student credit card got you through college—and held you down for a few years afterward—but isn't doing much for you now, it may be time for a new card that actually rewards you for purchases. Let's be clear that getting a new credit card for the rewards or bonus makes sense only if you pay your balance in full every month and never pay interest fees. Otherwise, it's not a reward because you're literally paying for it via fees.

When I got my first travel rewards credit card, I was beyond hyped for the sign-up bonus. It was something like 50,000 bonus miles if I spent $4,000 in the first ninety days. The problem was I generally spent only about $1,000 per month on credit. I was so tempted to spend extra money to hit that $4,000 mark, but it didn't make sense financially and I was trying to get a free flight—not a flight and more debt. So, I went on a mission to get the points without spending my own money.

Who was the first person to toss in my card for a group dinner? Me! Who accompanied family members to Costco and charged the haul in exchange for the cash? Me again! Who offered to pay for everything at work, filing expense reports within a day or two? Oh yes, also me. I did what I had to do to hit the target spending amount and get those bonus miles without incurring more debt, and I was so proud of myself. Those 50,000 miles got me a round-trip ticket to Puerto Rico with my college bestie, Safiyah. I had to pay only taxes and fees for that flight—it amounted to less than

$70. We had an amazing New Year's trip in 2015, just a few months before I became 100 percent debt-free!

If travel is not your thing, you might opt for a cash-back credit card instead. Cash back means you get a certain percentage of money back for each dollar you spend on your card. Sometimes instead of dollars, cash back comes in points, which you redeem in an online marketplace the credit card company offers through their app or website. So how do the percentages work? Let's say you have a card with a cash-back rate of 2 percent on all purchases, and you make a $100 purchase. You therefore earn $2 back in your account, so it's as if you paid only $98 instead of $100 when you went shopping.

If you're not sure which rewards make sense for you, look at your bank statements to see where you spend the most money. When I worked at a private company, I spent a lot at restaurants because I often paid for client dinners and then expensed them by completing a form to get reimbursed by the company. At that time, my card with 3 percent cash back on restaurant purchases was a sweet deal! Since the company was paying for the dinners, I was getting free meals *and* free money. A $200 dinner tab put an entrée and appetizer in my belly, plus $6 in my pocket!

It's tough to find a card that'll give you a fixed amount of cash back on all purchases, but some do exist for consumers with excellent credit. It's more likely you'll find cards that offer cash back on specific categories during certain periods of time, like restaurants this month and gas the next. Many cards have rotating categories that change every quarter, so pay attention and use the card strategically. One of my cards with rotating cash back at a 5 percent rate sends me an email every three months with a list of categories for that quarter.

Sometimes it's grocery stores. Other times it's transportation, including Amtrak and public transit. If I need to book a train for a work trip that's not for another few months, I'll go ahead and book it during that quarter to maximize my cash back.

I've narrowed down my credit card usage to one or two main cards that get me the most bang for my buck. Unless you're spending and paying back high amounts on your cards, spreading your purchases across too many cards makes it tough to accumulate any rewards at all because most cards require you to accumulate a certain amount of cash back before you can claim it. It's also tough to reach the most rewarding bonus levels on a travel rewards card if you don't use it consistently.

HOW TO READ YOUR CREDIT CARD STATEMENT

You don't need to read through your entire credit card statement word for word each month. I don't do that. You do need to know the top five key pieces of information on it and how to quickly scan the statement to find them. When it comes to credit cards, the words "statement" and "bill" are used interchangeably. A credit card statement is the same thing as a credit card bill. Some people even call it a statement bill. That's a bit weird to me, but anyway when I open my credit card statement in my banking app, I look for the same details: payment due date, statement cycle (also called billing period), total balance due, minimum payment due, and the amount I need to pay by the due date in order to avoid paying interest fees.

The first four pieces of information are super easy, because they're listed right on the bill. It's just a matter of looking in the same spot every month for those. On my credit card statement, the payment due date is at the top left corner of the page. The total balance shows up right below that date with the minimum payment just to the right of that. The opening and closing dates for the billing period are at the top right corner of the page in a much smaller font. Once you see your credit card bill a few times, you'll know exactly where to look for *your* key details.

The last piece of information is tricky! That's the amount I need to pay by the due date in order to avoid paying interest fees, and it's something I need to calculate based on my purchases during that billing period. As an example, let's say my statement has a due date of March 5, a total balance of $500, a minimum payment of $55, and the billing period is from January 10 through February 9. There are exactly thirty days in my billing period, so the next billing period starts on February 10. Any purchases I made during this thirty-day billing period must be paid in full by this bill's due date, which is March 5.

Okay, I got the first four pieces of information! Next, I scroll through my bill and notice that I spent $200 on Valentine's Day, which was February 14. That purchase was made *after* the last day of my billing period on February 9. My bill shows a total balance of $500, but to avoid interest fees I need to pay only $300 by March 5. The bank can't charge me yet for that $200 purchase since it was outside of this billing period. All purchases after my billing period ends will be accounted for in the next statement, which accounts for purchases in the next billing period starting on February 10.

If you pay for all your expenses in the billing period by the due date of that bill, you'll never pay interest fees. If you don't pay the full amount spent during your billing period by the due date on that bill, you're agreeing to pay interest fees on all the dollars you didn't pay back on time. These are the facts. Don't be fooled by the current balance due when you log on to see your statement. Do the simple math so you can avoid interest fees altogether. If you're not at this level yet, then at the very least, make sure your minimum payment is made on time for every bill.

BONUS HACK: USE IT, DON'T LOSE IT

Earlier, we established that closing a credit card, or having the bank close the card without your knowledge, negatively affects three credit factors that make up more than half of your total FICO score. So, what should you do if you're trying to stop using your credit cards so you can actually pay off your debt? Fortunately, there's an easy solution.

I have more than five credit cards, but I use only one or two for everyday purchases. Those would be the ones with the best travel rewards or highest cash-back perks. To prevent the other three cards from being closed for inactivity, I set up at least one recurring bill payment on each card. Then, I set up automatic bill payments from my checking account to all three credit cards. For example, I use my very first credit card to auto-pay my streaming service each month, and that keeps the card active and open. I don't use that card to pay for anything else at all. Auto-pay is set up to pay my credit card balance in full on the monthly due date, because I know the balance due is exactly what my streaming service costs, no more and no less.

Any bill you have that costs a fixed amount each month can be set up in this way! Money automatically moves from my checking account to that credit card, leaving a zero balance each month and never exceeding 10 percent of my total credit limit on that card. 1 set it up one time, and now 1 don't even have to do anything! This transaction happens in the background while 1 live my life. Creating an automated system by which your oldest cards still help you build credit even though you rarely use them is a game changer!

WHATEVER YOUR SITUATION

By learning the credit syllabus in this chapter and using it as a guide, you can boost your credit score to that "very good" or "excellent" range. Once you do that, you can begin to negotiate better deals like lower interest rates, higher credit limits, or waived annual fees. Use the info in this chapter to help you take steps to improve your credit as quickly as possible.

You don't need to put money toward credit repair. That's usually not a worthwhile expense, because it involves paying someone to remove inaccurate information from your credit report, and you can do that yourself. Also, if they can't repair your score or get you any results, they still charge you. Slick!

Once you have at least one credit card, flip it over and call the number on the back to speak with a customer service rep about your account. This is especially important if your interest rate is higher than the national average, which ranges from a 14 percent to 17 percent annual percentage rate (APR). If representatives are unresponsive, you can always say to them, "I've been getting a bunch of promotions in the mail from all these other credit card companies, and 1 keep ignoring them because 1 really like this card. But 1 noticed that some of these offers have significantly lower interest rates than 1 have on this card. Can you help me get a lower rate that's more in line with the offers I'm seeing in the mail?"

It's best not to cancel the card, because doing so will decrease your number of open accounts. It also hurts your age of credit and lowers your total credit available. Be relentless in achieving the credit score you want. Nobody will ever care more about your financial situation than you do!

PART 2

—

BE THE
CHANGE

TIME TO TAKE ACTION!

CHAPTER 5

Get Out of Debt
Your Way

IN SEPTEMBER 2017, I WAS WAITING FOR THE BUS WHEN
Mami called me in tears to tell me Papi had been admit-
ted to the hospital. He felt excruciating pain in his lower
abdomen. Doctors performed an endoscopy, sending a tiny
camera inside his body to look at his internal organs. After
work, I visited him in the hospital. The nurses and doctors
made one thing very clear: Papi's poor diet caused all of his
pain and problems.

Like many immigrants, my parents stuck with the eating
habits of their native country after moving to the United
States. We were raised on rice, beans, chicken, and *tostones*
(fried plantains). This meal is a staple in every traditional
Dominican home. You might notice nothing green is
included in this meal. Mami sometimes added iceberg let-
tuce, tomatoes, and, on a good week, sliced avocado, but Papi
rarely ate a side salad. He rarely ate any fiber at all.

Papi was diagnosed with diverticulitis, a condition involving inflammation or infection of small pouches in the walls of the digestive tract. The good news was that it's not a genetic disorder that would significantly impact his quality of living. It was all a result of Papi's poor diet! His was not a mild case, so he had to undergo surgery. The doctors made it clear, though, if he focused on rest, improved his diet, and took some antibiotics, he'd get better. The challenge was getting him to incorporate more high-fiber foods into his diet! The doctor gave us a list of recommended foods as well as foods Papi needed to avoid so he could recover after surgery. You can probably guess which list contained all his favorite foods!

Papi put in an ambitious effort for the first few weeks, eating greens and salads, mixing in vegetables, and having fish soup. But after some time, he started to cheat. When I went to visit my family, I'd find him by the grill, sneakily nibbling on pieces of fried chicken or crispy beef. We tried hard to support and encourage his healthful eating habits, but that worked only when he was home all day, because Mami could keep a close eye on him and monitor his meals.

After years of working late nights in the restaurant industry, Papi decided to become a taxi driver for more flexible hours. He liked coming and going as he pleased, taking breaks anytime he needed, and most of all, being outdoors and not standing over a hot stove! After dropping off clients in multiple neighborhoods, Papi would stop somewhere for lunch. Of course, he could've ordered soup or a salad, but he didn't. Papi craved food from hole-in-the-wall Latin restaurants serving a giant $7 plate of rice and beans with piles of meat, and no greens.

In December 2019, after another hospital scare, we learned Papi's condition had worsened. He was told very clearly, in front of his family, that his diet was the number one predictor of his health and life expectancy. What else did Papi need to hear to change his ways? I was so confused. Habits are so ingrained in us that we do them automatically with little to no thought. That means it's extremely challenging to change our habits. Papi had been stuck in his routine for more than sixty-five years. Such a long stretch of time makes it even *more* challenging to make a change!

We were determined to find out what motivates Papi. What means the world to him and inspires him to wake up and make a real effort, even on his toughest days? We realized his grandbabies are his whole world. Now that he was working fewer hours and approaching retirement, his own children were grown and off on their own. He got so much joy from spending time with his grandchildren.

One day my older sister told him, "Papi, you probably won't live to see your grandbabies graduate—not because of your age, but because of your poor food choices." We could tell he was deeply saddened by the idea that he might be taking away time from his life span—time he could spend with his precious grandbabies. Finally, someone had found his motivation. With tears in his eyes, Papi committed to changing his eating habits, even though he knew it would be difficult.

Papi still struggles with conforming to his diet, but as I write this his condition hasn't flared up for years. He also sees the doctor more regularly than before. Multiple surgeries, many prescriptions, and seemingly endless charts and print-outs had not scared him straight. Once my sister unlocked his internal motivation, though, we saw consistent effort on his part. He wanted to make changes, because he had his own goals and reasons.

I can relate to Papi's struggle with changing his eating habits. After all, I spent years trying to change my money habits so I could pay off my debt. I knew the struggle of wanting to change but not having the motivation to follow through. When faced with a problem in life, no matter its magnitude, it's always easier to stick your head in the sand and ignore it. The bigger the problem, the more insurmountable it might seem. Without something to keep you motivated on days when you most want to give up, it could feel like a hopeless case.

Just like planning your diet and lifestyle is a critical part of improving your physical health and stretching your life expectancy, making a plan to pay off your debt is critical to improving your financial health and stretching your money's life expectancy! Paying off debt is basically choosing to take actions that'll increase your financial net worth every week, month, or season. Let's go over five key steps that helped me increase my financial net worth and create sustainable money habits.

STEP 1: FIND YOUR ROOT WHY

People often use different words to describe the same thing. Some might say "find your mission or motivation," while others say "find your purpose." I prefer to say "find your *why*." Regardless of what you choose to call it, you need to identify yours. Identify your reason for wanting to improve your finances—*why* you want to improve your financial habits.

When you commit to the process of paying off debt, know that it can be lengthy. At times you'll feel stuck and just want to give up. You can always automate your minimum payments and keep spending as you normally do. *Most people won't even know.* They won't, but you will. You'll likely end up feeling even more stuck as a result of not taking action since you won't experience any momentum. The only way to get unstuck is to find your "Root Why."

A person's Root Why motivates them to put in the hard work daily, even when no one is watching them. Your Root Why comes from your vision for your life—how you want it to look and feel, regardless of what it's like right now. Find your Root Why by continuing to ask yourself one question: *Why?!*

Ask yourself questions like these:

- Why do I want to get my money right?
- Why was I motivated to read this book?
- Why have I felt satisfaction or fulfillment in the past?

Then apply your answers to another layer of *why* questioning to get to your Root Why. A meaningful answer to any of these questions tends to include some emotional motivation for the work you want to do. Here's an example of my Root Why process:

- *Why do I want to pay off my credit card debt?* Because...I'm sick and tired of paying high-interest fees.
- *Why am I tired of paying these interest fees?* Because...I never have any money left to take care of myself or my loved ones after my bills are paid.
- *Why do I want to do more for myself and my loves ones?* Because...I know my grandparents and parents couldn't go beyond paying bills and keeping their children fed, and I want to discontinue that vicious cycle.
- *Why don't I want to continue that cycle?* Because...con-

tinuing it means I'm actively choosing the cycle over empowering myself and my community.

- *Why does the prospect of choosing the cycle bother me?* Because...it means I'm willingly complicit in perpetuating a generational cycle of poverty. *Wow.*

Keep asking *why* until you get to *wow.* I refuse to be complicit in perpetuating the generational cycle of poverty in my family. That is my Root Why.

Your Root Why is your reminder that you're willing to consistently put in the work for something bigger than you, even though it might not be easy. You'll know you've found your Root Why when sacrifices that sounded insane to Past You are now seen as temporary hurdles along your deeply rewarding journey. You'll be willing to give up things you thought you'd never give up. Your Root Why is what it's all about!

STEP 2: FACE YOUR NUMBERS

Money is represented by numbers, and numbers represent math. Money equals math. You can't avoid the math of money! You just need to embrace that. The math involved in money management is generally simple, because it doesn't get more complicated than the four core operations: addition, subtraction, multiplication, and division. To do the math and face your numbers, you need a debt tracker for all debts you currently owe so you can put all your data in one place. Draw it on a piece of paper or pull up a spreadsheet—whatever works for you!

The format doesn't matter. What matters is that you commit to finding out exactly how much you owe and the interest rate for each loan. This might seem simple, but it can be emotionally challenging, especially if you have a high amount of debt, lots of different accounts, or a particularly negative relationship with money. Approach this step as if you were a detective solving a mystery.

First, collect all the facts! Don't get swallowed up by frustration or any negativity associated with the situation. Your chart should have four columns: Debt Name, Remaining Balance, Minimum Payment, and Interest Rate. Fill these in for each of your debt accounts. You might need to dig a little to find some of these details, such as the specific interest rate of a loan. You can find the balance and minimum payment due on your statement or bill, and you can call the lender for any details you can't find in your online account.

This step is critical in getting a big-picture view of your debt situation. It's data collection, so be prepared to pull up financial records or call your lenders if there's a detail you can't find in your account or on your statements. Banks and other lenders don't make it easy for you to find the information you need to understand your debt. I had so much trouble finding the interest rates for my credit cards. While I eventually found the interest rate in a tiny font size at the bottom of the last page of my credit card bill, it felt like I'd opened a *Where's Waldo?* book!

Once you have all the details filled in for each debt, add up the total amount you owe and fill that in at the bottom of your chart. For a lot of people, this can be the scariest part. It was extremely scary for me. It was the first time I saw just how far out of control my debt situation had gotten. I had gone from $1,500 on one credit card to $20,000 across multiple cards in just a few years. This is one experience that made me feel like the financial system was designed to keep consumers confused. They didn't want to make it clear, because as long as I remained in the dark about my 22 percent compounding interest rate, it benefitted the lender. The longer I was in debt, the more money my lenders made from interest payments.

It wasn't until the year 1989 that the "Schumer box" mentioned in the Truth in Lending Act took effect. This required credit card fees and terms to be printed in an easy-to-read, standardized format at the top of monthly statements.[45] Senator Chuck Schumer was the politician who advocated for this legislation, so now you know how the Schumer box got its name. These disclosures make clear the cost of interest and the total amount you'll pay over time if you pay only the minimum balance each month. Many people who don't understand this end up paying double or triple the amount of interest they'd expected to pay.

This viral tweet, which Sarah Kelly (@thesarahkelly) posted in September 2020, shows how compounding interest accruing over many years can get out of control: "I borrowed $38,876 for school from one private lender. Since graduating, I've paid that lender $31,501. How much do I still owe? $47,023."[46] Unfortunately, only certain student loans are included in the Truth in Lending Act. As of 2022, the average American owes about $102,000 for credit card balances, student loans, mortgages, and more.[47] Looking over your own

---

45   Fair Credit and Charge Card Disclosure Act of 1988, Pub. L. No. 100-583, 102 Stat. 2960 (1988); Charles E. Schumer, "Federal Reserve Board Approves 'Schumer Box' Truth in Lending Regulations," press release, September 28, 2000, https://web.archive.org/web/20090208170124/http://schumer. senate.gov/1-Senator%20Schumer%20Website%20Files/pressroom/press_releases/PR00315.html.

46   Sarah Kelly (@thesarahkelly), "I borrowed $38,876 for school from one private lender. Since graduating, I've paid that lender $31,501. How much do I still owe? $47,023," Twitter, September 2, 2020, 2:49 p.m., https://twitter.com/thesarahkelly/status/1301276120709505024.

47   Chris Horymski, "Average Consumer Debt Levels Increase in 2022," Experian, February 24, 2023, https://www.experian.com/blogs/ask-experian/research/consumer-debt-study/.

numbers can show you where you are financially compared to the average in America.

Calculate your average interest rate by adding up the interest rates across all your debts and dividing that amount by the total number of debts you owe. This sum is a key figure, because as you know the interest rate you pay on debt is determined by your credit score. So, if you're paying a higher-than-average interest rate (anything in the double digits is considered high), consider applying some hacks from the credit syllabus in Chapter 4. The hacks help boost your credit score so you might qualify for a low-interest rate loan to pay off all your debts so you have just one monthly payment to make to a new lender.

We talk more about this option, called loan consolidation, at the end of this chapter. Most people carrying high amounts of debt tend to be in the dark about their total balance or how much interest they're paying. They either choose not to do the math or push it to the back of their mind because they're too afraid to look at the numbers. When you don't confront your fear, you allow that fear to control you. We know that in order to do better, you first need to *know* better. The knowledge comes first, and the action follows.

STEP 3: FIND YOUR TRIBE

Once you're committed to paying off debt, there's no need to make the commitment even harder than it already is! If everyone around you is spending money to shop, take vacations, and go to concerts, it might be harder for you to reject those social pressures and temptations to save money instead. You don't need to deprive yourself of everything that brings you joy.

If you deprive yourself of everything you love, you might quickly lose sight of your Root Why and wallow in misery. Deprivation doesn't motivate most people, but community and connection does! Finding the right tribe of people who are on the same page as you about creating a financially healthy lifestyle and increasing their financial net worth is a game changer!

Your tribe can be made up of people you know in your life, people you know only from the internet, or both! You don't have to limit your tribe to people you've already met. The top reason for me to find a tribe of like-minded people was for accountability and inspiration. I found those people on social media! As I shared in Chapter 1, posting my #moneygoals on Instagram helped me stay motivated when I felt like quitting. I used social media as a resilience resource whenever I felt like everyone around me was living their best lives while I was struggling with debt. My tribe helped me bounce back.

I recognize that plenty of people on social media compare themselves to others who have more financial resources, and that's not healthy. "Comparison is the thief of joy," as Theodore Roosevelt said. What if we were to stop comparing and start cheering? Since my YouTube channel and Instagram page are all about personal finance, my feed showed me posts from people worldwide who were also learning about money and dealing with their own financial journeys.

I loved seeing people post about their #moneygoals, so I unfollowed all the celebrities, blogs, media, comedians, and models I had been following. I was so focused on my Root Why that I blocked out anything that didn't contribute to helping me reach my goals. I replaced all that messiness with popular financial hashtags in my feed by following #debt-freejourney, #passiveincome, #nospendchallenge, and more.

Once I followed these hashtags, it was as if I were scrolling through a completely different dimension!

It felt as if I'd left the whack version of the internet and entered a new version where everyone was ambitious as hell! I was double-tapping financial quotes, messages, images, videos, and resources, and chatting with people who were on debt repayment journeys like mine. People posted about everything from debt repayment, creative saving strategies, and frugality to side hustles, investing, and entrepreneurship. I even found the behavioral economics nerds, who posted videos of Uncle Richie and Auntie Wendy! It felt like a breath of fresh financial air.

Finding my tribe of like-minded money nerds was the reason I successfully became debt-free. You may have heard this famous quote from *Don Quixote*: "Tell me what company you keep, and I will tell you what you are." Or maybe you're familiar with entrepreneur Jim Rohn's famous phrase: "You're the average of the five people you spend the most time with." The people I was devoting more time and energy to were inspiring me to bring up my average! Authors, bloggers, and video creators helped me become more ambitious, more knowledgeable, and more of a go-getter. I spent less time focusing on negative people and negativity in general. I took responsibility for my life and devoted more time to thinking about the lessons I was learning on my journey. This helped me create the new life I desired and deserved.

Eventually, I started attending in-person events and got to meet many of the amazing people whose faces I was so used to seeing on my phone. I attended FinCon, Elevate, Young Women and Money Conference, and many more! After being an attendee for a year, I applied to be a speaker at FinCon and was later invited to speak on the main stage.

I went from making social media connections to making real-life social connections that continue to help me out in life, even beyond money issues.

STEP 4: MAKE A PLAN (AND BACK IT UP)

When it comes to paying off debt, it's best not to be too attached to your plan. After all, life happens. Circumstances shift. So, plan for that ahead of time by creating a backup plan—Plan B.

Plan A is the one you'll use daily, weekly, and monthly—unless something unexpected happens, in which case you activate Plan B. Note that this step takes less than two minutes if you have the details in your chart from Step 2: Face Your Numbers. To make Plan A, type your numbers into an online debt payoff calculator—my absolute favorite is available for free at calculator.net. The site was created by a group of information technology professionals who believe quality tools for managing your finances (and your physical health) should be available to the public for free. Ooh, yes! I agree. The cool thing is that financial professionals from various advising firms have reviewed the site's calculators, so we can trust that they're legit.

Okay, it's time to crack your knuckles and get to work:

1. Pull up calculator.net.
2. Type keyword "debt" in the search bar.
3. Select the Debt Payoff Calculator.
4. Enter each Debt Name, Remaining Balance, Minimum Payment, and Interest Rate.
5. Add Extra Payments (beyond your minimum payments), if you can afford to.

Click the "Calculate" button to see how much time it will take you to pay off all your debt given the details you entered. You'll see the loans listed in order from highest interest rate to lowest. This prioritizes eliminating debt as quickly and as efficiently as possible.

You'll also see the number of months it will take you to pay off your debts, the dollar amount you'll pay in interest during that time, and the payment schedule, which is my favorite part! It takes just a few minutes to know exactly how much money you need to pay toward each debt, exactly when the payment amounts change, and exactly how long you'll make payments. I know of no easier way to make your debt payoff plan for free.

That was Plan A, which includes extra payments beyond the minimums required because you want to be aggressive on your journey to success! Add an extra monthly payment if you can afford to, or send a one-time extra payment per year. For example, if you get an income tax refund check, make an extra debt payment at that time. Many experts recommend homeowners pay one extra mortgage payment per year to save money on interest fees and pay off their mortgage a little sooner.

In an ideal world, we'd do all of that and more to get rid of debt faster and put that money to work for ourselves and our loved ones instead, but life happens. You need the option to quickly activate your backup plan. That's where Plan B comes in! The B stands for "bare minimum." That means don't include any extra payments in your debt payoff plan, paying only the minimum due for each account.

To create your Plan B, use the same calculator with all your details and simply remove any extra payments you listed. Press "Calculate" again to now see your slightly less aggressive Plan B. Choose whichever works for you and your financial situation, or toggle back and forth between the two plans throughout the year to your heart's desire.

The mainstream finance industry makes it seem like you have only two options when it comes to repaying debt: the Snowball method versus the Avalanche method. (We'll get to these next.) That's just not the case! Money comes with so much nuance, not to mention the intersection of money and our feelings about it. You may have to try different angles to test what works for you, and ultimately you need to do what's best for you and your loved ones. Only you know what's ideal for you.

While online financial tools are extremely helpful, they don't consider nuance. Some people, for example, will just never feel inspired by a plan that focuses only on the numbers. Before tackling Step 5, let's talk about how to deal with that.

SNOWBALL VERSUS AVALANCHE

When it comes to debt repayment strategies, there are two teams: Snowball and Avalanche. Both teams agree debts should be put in order from highest priority to lowest, and every account should have minimum payments on auto-pay. The teams disagree when it comes to how you should prioritize paying off the debts.

If you want to pay your debts in order from smallest balance to biggest, then you're Team Snowball. Your top-priority debt has the smallest remaining balance. That means any extra payments you can afford to make, after all the minimums are paid, go toward your smallest debt. The reasoning here is twofold. First, having several different loans at once can be overwhelming. Second, it feels good to eliminate one whole account right away. That instant gratification makes the dopamine go wild.

If you're like me, you prefer Team Avalanche. We prioritize paying debts in order from highest interest rate to lowest. Any extra money we get is sent directly to the debt with the highest interest rate. That's because, at the end of the day, we're motivated by data and saving the most dollars.

Remember, there's always room for nuance when it comes to money. Rather than choosing between these strategies, you can rep Team Hybrid. Leverage the best of both strategies by paying off the debt with the smallest balance first. Then, switch over to the debt with the highest interest rate once that account has a zero balance. Simply reorder all your debt accounts, placing highest priority on the one with the highest interest rate. Basically, you can cross the finish line with Team Avalanche, even if you started the race with Team Snowball.

Here's an example with four realistic debt amounts for everyday Americans. Let's say we have a discretionary $1,000 to put toward debt each month, and we owe a total of $41,800. This includes $800 for a medical bill; $10,000 for a student loan; $15,000 for a car loan; and $16,000 on a credit card.

Team Snowball won't even look at the interest rates. They put the debts in order from smallest to biggest, automating minimum payments for each one. Any extra money gets added toward the $800 medical bill until it's paid in full, since that's the smallest balance. Then, they take the money previously going toward the medical bill and add it to the minimum payment for the $10,000 student loan, which is next up in size order.

That creates a snowball effect on these monthly payments, which build upon themselves and get bigger. Keeping the minimum payments automated for the $15,000 car loan and $16,000 credit card, those on Team Snowball start making bigger payments on the student loan until the balance hits zero. Now, they have only the credit card getting a minimum payment, and all the rest of their money goes toward the car loan until the car is paid off. Finally, they take all the money and put it toward the biggest debt, which is the credit card.

Team Avalanche, on the other hand, asks for the interest rates right away. Let's say the $800 medical bill has 0 percent interest; the $10,000 student loan is at 5 percent; the $15,000 car loan is at 3 percent; and the $16,000 credit card is at 22 percent (ouch!). Team Avalanche puts the debts in order from highest interest rate to lowest, automating minimum payments on each account. Any extra money gets added to the $16,000 credit card until that's fully paid, since it's the highest rate debt.

Then, those on Team Avalanche take the money previously going toward the credit card and add it to the minimum payment for the $10,000 student loan, which is the next highest rate debt at 5 percent. This creates the same snowball effect on the monthly payments. They build upon themselves and get bigger, but they prioritize paying off higher interest debts first since they're the ones growing the fastest. Keeping the minimum payments automated for the $15,000 car loan and $800 medical bill, they now make bigger payments on the student loan until the balance hits zero.

Then, something cool happens! While they're focusing on the student loan, the $800 medical debt gets paid off because the balance was so small. That's right! Team Avalanche still gets a hit of dopamine—it's just not as immediate. Finally, they make one large monthly payment on the car loan until that's paid in full.

Assuming the credit card charges a minimum of 2 percent of the balance each month, and all other minimum balances are between $75 and $250, Team Snowball takes fifty-seven months and pays $14,656 in interest fees during that time for a total of more than $56,400 to become debt-free. Team Avalanche takes fifty-one months and pays $8,550 in interest fees for a total $50,350 to become debt-free. That's more than $6,000 in savings.

Why would anyone want to throw away $6,000 and take six months longer to get out of debt? Well, a lot of people believe they won't make it very far if they don't get the immediate gratification of eliminating one debt right away. They fear they'll lose motivation and give up too soon. I agree that what matters most is your motivation and commitment, and that's where your Root Why comes in. I don't recommend focusing so much on the balance to keep motivated. Your Root Why is the North Star guiding you and reminding you of the reason you're on this journey.

Keep in mind you can also choose Team Hybrid! You can start with Team Snowball for a few months until you eliminate your lowest debts, then switch over to Team Avalanche after you get that early win in the books. You just have to go back to the debt repayment calculator and create a new plan starting from that point forward. There are so many strategies you can use to stay motivated, and they're all rooted in making financial health feel fun. If you can find a way to change the environment around your debt payoff journey to make it genuinely enjoyable, you'll be far more likely to stick with it. Read on for a few suggestions.

CHART IT

Since my credit cards all had high interest rates, I joined Team Avalanche. The psychological benefits Team Snowball likes to brag about caught my attention, though. I thought about my classroom teaching days, designing a system that would show me my progress and give me benchmarks to celebrate. This was how I tracked my fourth graders' reading growth and math achievement, and it worked like a charm.

Since my total debt was $20,000, I made a chart with twenty boxes—one for every $1,000 owed. Each time my total debt decreased by $1,000, I placed a Post-it note over a new box. You could also color in the boxes or fill them with cute stickers, if you're feeling extra festive or artistic. The point is to create something physical that makes your achievements active and tactile.

This is especially helpful for Team Avalanche and Team Hybrid because, even though you're not entirely focused on eliminating debt accounts, you're eliminating small increments of debt. This visual reminder helps you stay inspired along the road to your big goal. Something this simple goes a long way toward keeping you motivated because it infuses a fun little ritual!

TREAT YO' SELF

This is the same idea as the chart, but you add in a little treat. If you love going to the movies, say, but have cut back on that to aggressively pay down debt, treat yourself to a matinee every time you meet a benchmark. Or maybe you're like me and love getting a massage, so do that instead. Make the reward unique and special, but do it only when you meet your benchmarks! Otherwise, it won't feel like a treat at all. It'll be another day in the life, and that's not very motivating.

Set up the same chart as before. Grab some Post-it notes, and jot down some things you want to do or buy. Write on the sticky side so you can't see the reward when it's on the wall. Cover your chart with Post-its, and each time you reach a new benchmark, peel one off and treat yo' self. This also makes for great social media content you can share, if you're into publicly posting your progress like I am.

PAIR IT WITH JOY

Even after you create your Plan A and Plan B, it's a long journey so staying on track with your debt payments can feel repetitive and mundane. When I started paying off debt, I set up auto-payments on all my credit cards, but I manually made the extra payment toward my highest rate card each week. I logged into the online portal and typed in the extra payment amount then submitted it. I tried to make my extra payment around the same time on the same day, so it felt like my own little money ritual. To make it a positive experience that I looked forward to rather than dreaded, I paired up the payment with what I love to do: visit my family!

I get so much joy from spending time with my loud-laughing family, especially because I'm *la tía favorita*—the favorite aunt! In mid-2014, when I was a few months into my debt payoff journey, my sister became a new mom to the cutest twins ever. On Friday nights, I walked over to Sandra's house to see my baby nephews and have a glass of wine. I made a deal with myself that I couldn't leave my apartment until I made my extra weekly payment first. By pairing something I didn't love doing (making payments) with something that brought me joy (snuggling babies), I tricked my mind into thinking they were both part of my joyful Friday routine.

For printable progress charts you can use to stay motivated, and more creative ideas beyond those shared here, download your free guide at mindyourmoneybook.com.

STEP 5: PREPARE FOR FAILURE

I know you're probably thinking, *Failure? She means "prepare for success," right?* Nope. I mean "prepare for failure" because failure is part of success. Who doesn't want to taste sweet success? By default, we plan and prepare for success. Now we just need to tack on one itty-bitty, but incredibly important, change along the way. We must accept the fact that we will fail at times on the road to success. We'll likely fail more than once because we're only human, and the debt payoff process isn't easy.

Imagine what a moment of failure will look like, sound like, and feel like for you. This is called negative visualization. It's when you imagine that a negative outcome or worst-case scenario actually happens. This may sound odd because social media is oversaturated with messages about positivity, abundance, and manifestation. All those things are amazing. We should practice those consistently, but there needs to be room to create the mental strength for overcoming failure when it arrives.

Negative visualization is not practiced daily, but rather once or twice before embarking on your journey. You revisit it only when you need to. To be clear, you're not planning for failure, but you will be prepared for its inevitability at intervals along your path. You'll know exactly what to do when failure arises.

When I started making payments toward my debt, I created a budget that allowed me to set aside more than $300 per week for credit card payments. (We talk more about budgeting in Chapter 6.) It was painful, but I was determined to get rid of my debt in eighteen months. I came home from work, feeling exhausted, and I was often tempted to order delivery instead of eating food I had at home. On other days, I reflected on how bad my week was and felt enticed to do some online shopping to feel better.

Sometimes the temptation got me, and I fell off. It happened multiple times, but I never gave up! I may have been derailed by temptation, exhaustion, and Amazon, but I didn't quit. I kept going even after failing over and over again, because I'd already visualized failure as part of my journey. Negative visualization involves writing down sentences you can read out loud whenever you consider quitting. I call these "I will" statements. They're framed like this: *When (A) happens, I will (B).* Here are some examples:

When I'm exhausted and don't stick to the plan, I will post on social media, admitting that I messed up and recommitting to my debt payoff plan.

When I skip a week or a month of executing my plan, I will call my best friend and explain what happened. I will ask her to check in on me for the next few weeks to help me be accountable for getting back on track.

When an emergency comes up that causes me to change my debt payoff plan, I will tap my emergency savings fund, then readjust my plan and share it with my tribe.

Including negative visualization as an early step in your debt payoff journey ensures you won't be shocked or ill prepared when you fail. Being shocked can trigger a physiological response called "fight, flight, or freeze." The last thing you want to do is run away from your debt or take no action at all. The reason we make a plan is because we have success in mind. The best way to ensure you'll get to success is to know ahead of time what you'll say and do when failure rears its ugly little head.

Just think of how devastated I would've been if I had never considered failure at all. Think of the disappointment of experiencing failure for the first time. Think of the shock of not knowing what to say or do. Negative visualization is how you limit the impact of devastation, disappointment, or shock by training your mind for the challenge before it arrives. You won't be bummed out or mad at yourself, and you can just get back to business.

Schedule at least ten minutes for your negative visualization exercise. Write down the #moneygoals you're working toward and include specific numbers, such as dollar amounts and payment dates. Oh, look at that! You already crunched the exact numbers and mapped out your payment dates in Step 4: Make a Plan (and Back It Up). Pull up that plan, and look over it for a few minutes. Picture yourself making payments and sticking to the plan. Then answer the following questions in writing:

1. How would you feel if you found out you were no longer able to achieve this plan?
2. List the people, places, or actions that motivate you to get back on track with your plan when you get derailed.
3. Write down three or more "I will" statements to read aloud and call yourself to action when you fail. *When (A) happens, I will (B).*

This is a simple and incredibly powerful exercise. When you prepare for failure, you reframe failure. You no longer associate it with fear or shame, and instead you see it as an opportunity to try again. Writing your "I will" statements is Current You creating an invitation for Future You to continue trying. This is incredibly inspiring for most people. However, a few might still believe they truly can't do it on their own.

If no debt payoff resources or tips in this chapter are helpful to you, consider credit counseling or filing for bankruptcy. Those have negative implications for your credit report, so you should always first explore all other options, including loan consolidation. For a list of my recommended resources for credit counseling or navigating bankruptcy, download the free guide at mindyourmoneybook.com.

LOAN CONSOLIDATION

Debt consolidation is when you take out a new loan and use that loan money to pay off all your existing debts. A consolidation loan offers a fixed monthly payment amount with either a lower overall interest rate compared to your current debts or a rate equal to the average interest rate of your current debts. This type of loan is especially helpful for people juggling multiple high-interest debts at once. Keeping track of debts with different rates, due dates, and balances can feel overwhelming.

Loan consolidation helps you simplify your finances so you owe just one monthly payment to one lender. If you're willing to pay more in the long run to get a smaller monthly payment amount, you can select a longer repayment term. However, if you want to pay the least amount of interest and be done as quickly as possible, then you should choose a shorter repayment term and pay a bit more per month.

Don't get too excited though. You have to qualify for these loans based on your credit score, and the application leads to a hard inquiry on your credit report. *Womp!* Lenders also want to see the ratio of how much debt you owe relative to how much income you earn. That's why it was so hard for my friend's little sister to get a consolidation loan when I was a cosigner for her student loan back in the day.

You also have to keep an eye out for unnecessary fees that come with these types of loans. For example, some lenders charge an origination fee ranging from 1 percent to 6 percent of the principal amount borrowed. This fee is taken right out of the amount you borrow so you'll get less money in your bank account as a result. You already know how important it is to comparison shop for bank accounts. It's no different with debt consolidation services. If you decide a debt consolidation loan is what you need, shop around for the best lender and make sure unnecessary fees don't keep you in debt longer.

The most important thing is to keep trying. Don't quit! I wish there were a single guaranteed plan or strategy that would work for you no matter what. That's just not how life works. Life is all trial and error, so try and try again.

Next up, we talk about different budgeting methods to find one that works for you.

CHAPTER 6

Budget Better

WE LIVE IN A TIME WHEN COMPANIES AND SOCIAL MEDIA platforms know more about where and when we spend our dollars than we do. Google, Amazon, and Facebook know exactly what you buy, where you shop, and what decisions went into the process. Every time you search, share a post, comment, or like, they keep track. They know your zip code, which informs your standard of living. They know whether you drive a car, take public transportation, walk past stores, or drive to them. They know what music you listen to and what shows you stream.

Why is everything we do tracked online? That's easy. Information about how and where people spend money is the most valuable commodity in today's marketplace. Data makes dollars! So much money is made by tracking what you buy, then targeting and retargeting you with links to similar purchases.

In the first four months of 2022, the top ten advertisers on TikTok spent more than $126 million on ads.[48] They spend

---

48 Pathmatics, *The State of TikTok Advertising in the U.S.* (San Francisco: Sensor Tower, 2022), 5, https://go.sensortower.com/rs/351-RWH-315/images/state-of-tiktok-advertising-report-2022.pdf.

even more to develop algorithms that track consumer data and to lobby against privacy protection laws that get in the way of their data-mining schemes. It's not only online, either. Some grocery stores use Bluetooth to track your phone down the aisles and find out where you linger and what items you pick up.

Here's my question: if Facebook and Google are so desperate for your data, why aren't you? They're doing a great job trying to take your money. You have to do a better job trying to keep it. How do you collect data about your spending to make sure you're doing the best you can with what you've got? Here's a hint: it starts with a B.

BUDGETING

I've worked with so many people who say they have a budget but still struggle with money. To be honest, that's a red flag for me. You have a budget, but *do you budget?* Budgeting is a process you use consistently to make sure you don't spend more than you make. If you don't keep track, you'll lose track. It's simple, but it ain't easy. I'm a big fan of automating the whole process through the anti-budget.

THE ANTI-BUDGET

Paula Pant popularized the anti-budget on her platform *Afford Anything.* Her blog and podcast focus on pursuing financial independence and real estate investing. I highly recommend tuning in because she drops real gems and interviews some remarkable people. In a 2013 blog post about the anti-budget, she wrote this:

"There's no need to track how much you're spending on

groceries, electricity, restaurants and clothes. You don't need to line-item your sunglasses, toothpaste, and that time you dropped $80 at the bar."[49]

Her process involves deciding how much you want to save, pulling that amount off the top, and "relaxing" about the rest. Yep, she uses the word relaxing to describe budgeting!

Most people are allergic to budgeting, because of all the old-school financial advice dominating the personal finance sector—you know, the male, pale, stale stuff. "Track every dollar!" There's actually an app called EveryDollar. "Don't leave a penny uncategorized in your zero-based budget Excel spreadsheet!" Or you're told to get all your cash out of the ATM for the month and stuff it into envelopes like our *abuelitas* (grandmas) did.

A small percentage of the population religiously uses one or more of these budgeting methods, and it works for them. I was one of those people back in the day. But that doesn't mean I enjoyed it. For me, it was like doing chores or typing a twenty-page paper in college. It needed to get done, so I'd suck it up and do it. Most of the time I had to lie to myself and pretend it wasn't so bad. The little voice in my head sounded like a creepy horror movie character. *This isn't boring. This isn't tedious. You like doing this.*

When you're just focused on creating and maintaining a perfect budget every week or month, you risk missing the whole forest for some dry trees. Paula's blog popped up on my Facebook feed in 2018, after four years of tracking every cent I earned and spent with a zero-based budget. Her blog post fundamentally changed the way I think about budgeting, helping me develop my own version of the anti-budget.

49   Paula Pant, "Hate Budgeting? Here's the Easiest Budget Ever," *Afford Anything* (blog), March 5, 2013, https://affordanything.com/anti-budget-or-80-20-budge/.

To start, I pulled up my spending from the previous few months to calculate the total amount of money I had spent on fixed expenses versus variable ones. Fixed expenses don't change from month to month: rent or mortgage payments, transportation costs, internet and utility bills, phone bills, loan payments, credit card minimums, streaming services, subscriptions, and more. Variable expenses are bills that vary depending on the month. For example, we tend to spend way more on food and shopping during the holidays and for birthdays. Other variable expenses include personal care, travel, entertainment, medical costs, and so on. Finally, there are expenses most people should prioritize but typically don't, such as savings, investments, and insurance.

I split these expenses, whether variable or fixed, into two categories: needs and wants. Netflix and Spotify are fixed expenses, but they sure ain't necessary! I wrote down my total monthly income and subtracted all the expenses I considered to be needs. To make sure I didn't skip out on savings and investments, I marked those as needs, too. The amount left was for me to use freely. I could use it for anything I listed as a want, or anything else I didn't expect or plan for.

For variable needs, I calculated the average amount I spent over the previous few months of budgeting and used that amount. I went from having a bunch of categories and rules to just one flexible spending amount. Then, *voila!* No more budgeting rigidly into a spreadsheet. No more predetermined spending amounts for every little thing. No more guilt when spending money on whatever I want.

I was lucky to have already been budgeting for years before I started my anti-budget. If you don't have all the data from your previous few months of budgeting, it might take you a little bit longer to set this up, but you'll only have to do it once. You can come back to it if your income changes or your expenses change, but that's usually only a few times a year.

It's critical at first to dedicate time to track your spending and analyze those expenses so you know exactly what you typically spend money on every month. This gives you a reality check to cut back in areas where you may be mindlessly overspending. You may underestimate some strong spending habits and how your mind justifies unnecessary or frivolous spending. You often know you should get your hands on the reins, but you don't. Let's change that!

AUTOMATE IT

Anti-budgeting is easiest when it's fully automated, because you don't have to actively do anything aside from your daily spending decisions. It's even better when paired with Auntie Wendy's research, which I shared in Chapter 2. A large amount at the beginning of the month can give a false sense of abundance, so it's best to get paid in smaller, more frequent payments.

First, divide the flexible spending amount by four weeks in a month. Next, set up a weekly recurring payment from your Main Money account to your Fun Money account. If you use debit cards for spending, this is all you need to do and it's super easy! If you use credit cards for purchases, prevent overspending by paying off all your credit cards weekly. That way there's no money in your Fun Money account that's meant for your credit card bills.

Here's a sample budget for a monthly income of $4,000 with needs totaling $3,120, or 78 percent of earnings.

- $320 for emergency savings fund (8 percent of income)
- $400 for a Roth IRA investment account (10 percent of income)
- $1,300 for rent (32.5 percent of income)
- $260 for utility bills and internet (6.5 percent of income)
- $80 for cell phone bill (2 percent of income)
- $320 for food (8 percent of income)
- $190 for student loan (4.7 percent of income)
- $250 for car payment (6.3 percent of income)

That leaves $880 for absolutely anything this person wants. This could be an automated weekly transfer of $220 or a bi-weekly transfer of $440. There are no rigid guidelines about how to use this money, because they've already saved, invested, and paid the bills by pulling that off the top. If you're someone who's accustomed to being a bit messy with money, or you overspend and carry debt often, it'll take a few paychecks to get adjusted to this new system. The initial transition might feel a little painful, because you can't trick the anti-budget.

If you set it up correctly, there's no way to spend more than you earn. Stay focused on hitting your monthly financial goals, such as reducing debt, saving, and investing. It'll get easier and more flexible as time goes on, as you practice curation, and as you learn what does and doesn't matter most to you. You'll make some tough choices, but eventually the system runs itself like a well-oiled machine. All you had to do is put a few structures in place in the very beginning of your anti-budget venture.

The financial advice shared here is most applicable for full-time employees, but if you don't have steady income, you can still adapt. Your finances might be a little trickier to automate if your income is sporadic, so plan to build in time weekly for some manual tasks related to your finances. First, figure out the bare minimum amount of money you need to get by in a week. Then, manually transfer it to your Fun Money account on the same day weekly.

Why would anyone do this manually? Well, if there's a week when money is extra tight you might not always have reliable funds in your Main Money account to allow for an automatic recurring transfer to be processed. You may need to lean on a credit card until you book a few more gigs and bring in some extra cash. On the flip side, maybe you have amazing weeks or months when you bring in lots of extra money from picking up additional gigs. In that case, you should leave that money in your Main Money account or transfer it to a high-yield savings account for longer term savings goals.

The point is to get in the habit of saving more when your income spikes, and rely on your savings to hold you down when you experience a drop in income. You don't have to forever forget about any extra money you make. Try to pretend extra money didn't come in until you have at least a few months of living expenses stacked in your high-yield savings account for an emergency. Trust me—you'll be so glad you did, during a future week when money is tight, or when unexpected costs pop up to surprise you. Either way, Future You will thank you.

SCARCITY MINDSET

I honestly wish I had found Paula's blog sooner because I would've had an awareness that there are ways to manage money that aren't rooted in a scarcity mindset. Scarcity means you view your resources, such as money and food, as limited. Rather than meticulously subtracting each expense from my budget every week or month, I shifted my approach to adding up my spending until I reached the weekly spending goal. If money was left in my account, it rolled over to the next week or month, and that felt amazing!

Adding up your expenses rather than subtracting them from your income when budgeting is a key difference that helps you move away from a scarcity mindset so you can take strides toward abundance. Adding is rooted in abundance, while subtracting is rooted in scarcity. When you operate from a place of abundance, you believe you have access to enough resources, or more than enough, to cover your needs and wants.

In Alicia Keys's autobiography, *More Myself*, she shares the story of her first big paycheck. She let the money sit in her account for weeks and couldn't bring herself to spend a dime. Why? She'd spent her entire life traumatized by poverty and feared losing it all at any point. While shopping with her childhood friend, she returned all the items she'd picked out after learning the purchase price totaled more than $3,000. She was eventually convinced to buy two of those items as a celebration of her hard work and success, but ultimately this experience taught her she'd been making financial decisions from a place of feeling lack.

Scarcity mindset typically manifests itself in experiences like this. People focus so much on what they don't have that they can't spend without guilt when they do have money. Scarcity mindset has gotten a bad rap on social media, especially in the area of personal finance. Real talk though— having a scarcity mindset is not all bad!

Money in any given society needs to be somewhat scarce

because if there were an unlimited supply, it would be worthless. We're constantly told to get rid of the scarcity mindset and shift to an abundance mindset, but if your new mindset is based on a false sense of abundance, then it's a terrible idea. No, I'm not advocating for 100 percent scarcity mindset and zero abundance, but modern financial conveniences trick us into thinking money isn't scarce when it is.

To make purchases, I can use cash, gift cards, debit cards, credit cards, mobile wallets on my phone or digital watch, or payment apps, or I can apply for a personal loan. I can also wire the money. And if I don't have enough cash in my checking account, I can use a "buy now, pay later" service and still get what I want right away. Buy now, pay later, or BNPL, is a type of loan that allows you to pay for a bigger purchase in four smaller equal amounts either weekly, bi-weekly, or monthly. These services are often interest-free, which is especially attractive to younger generations who tend to be more fearful of high interest rate credit card debt. The problem is that missed payments lead to costly late fees and may negatively impact your credit score if they end up in collections.

Have I mentioned that there's always room for nuance when it comes to money? A healthy awareness of your limitations helps you keep yourself in check and forces you to be resourceful, not resourceless. Making do with what you've got is a critical life skill as you learn to persevere through less-than-ideal circumstances. How do we maintain a healthy awareness of scarcity without fully adopting a scarcity mindset? It's all in how you perceive your spending choices. The anti-budget pulls you away from penny-pinching to introduce you to curation.

By the end of high school, my dream was to become a

famous museum curator. I was a paid intern at the Studio Museum in Harlem for most of 2005. While more than 80 percent of museum leadership positions are held by White professionals in America, I witnessed the leadership of both Dr. Lowery Stokes Sims and Thelma Golden, two Black women who are among the baddest in the NYC art game.[50] I never considered becoming an art curator until then. There's limited space to display art in galleries and museums, so the curator's job is to decide which pieces to exhibit.

You're the curator of your life. As humans we have an insatiable appetite for stuff, and we're rarely satisfied. We want it all, and we don't want to choose! Imagine trying to appreciate art in a gallery completely covered in paintings from floor to ceiling and wall to wall. As a matter of fact, you don't have to imagine. Just search online for images of "Paris salons," and you'll see the tacky, maximalist "more is more" aesthetic of the Victorian era. It might make you feel like the vomiting emoji.

That's how it feels when you don't curate your money choices. To help you get started, I created a free template you can download to walk through each step of automating your anti-budget. I even include video clips and articles from my favorite financial creators to help you find the right balance between scarcity mindset and abundance mindset. Check out your free guide, with these resources and more, at mindyourmoneybook.com.

---

50 Roger Schonfeld and Mariët Westermann, *Art Museum Staff Demographic Survey* (New York: The Andrew W. Mellon Foundation, 2015), 7–9, https://mellon.org/media/filer_public/ba/99/ba99e53a-48d5-4038-80e1-66f9ba1c020e/awmf_museum_diversity_report_aamd_7-28-15.pdf.

When you have more purchases to make than money to cover them, thoughts of deprivation sneak up inside your mind. Quickly kick them out! Focus on welcoming abundance by saying, "I'm curating my life to reduce scarcity and increase my standard of living." I've lost count of how many times I've had to check myself and actively work on shifting my mindset.

One of the most common questions people ask about my budget is this: "To pay off your debt, did you earn more or cut back your spending budget?" The answer is...both!

When I first calculated all my minimum payments, I couldn't afford the monthly total. It's no wonder I kept using my credit cards to pay my utility bills, and the interest fees just kept growing. In Chapter 1, I mention how I creatively earned more money by doing artsy side hustles like selling purses on Etsy and eyebrow threading. Simultaneously, I was going over my spending with a fine-tooth comb because I had just read Suze Orman's *Women and Money*. In the book she suggests looking at your spending for problematic patterns, and that's exactly what I did.

I printed out three months of banking and credit card statements, and examined each of my purchases—something I had never done before. The most I'd ever done was glance over a credit card bill, but that reflected only about thirty days of spending, not ninety. It was the most eye-opening way to get a picture of where my money was going. If you've never done this before, I urge you to print out your last three credit card and bank statements. Grab some highlighter pens, and look over every penny you've spent.

Looking through my spending made me hyperaware of my spending patterns. When the data was staring me right in the face, I could no longer deny I was part of my own problem. The data painted such a clear story of my money habits. I realized why Google and Facebook go to such great lengths to collect our data! I saw constant purchases of snacks at different bodegas or at Dunkin Donuts. I saw CVS, Walgreens, H&M, Old Navy, Target, and Amazon—far more than I expected.

I looked around my apartment and peeped at all the lotion bottles, candles, and random little trinkets I'd bought whenever I was out and about, shopping, or running to CVS just because I was bored or wanted a pick-me-up. It was death by a thousand cuts! A lot of financial experts call these "budget leaks."

A daily purchase from Dunkin or Starbucks is not the sole reason I got into $20,000 of credit card debt, and I'm not here to shame anyone for their daily morning coffee or other small spending splurge. One of the most important parts of this exercise is to remove any judgment. If you allow that little voice in your head to say mean things, the exercise will not help you at all. It might help to pretend you're looking at your friend's spending patterns—preferably a friend you treat kindly. (You should treat all your friends kindly, but that's none of my business.) Use any tricks you need to keep yourself honest and positive.

In my case all the micro-purchases were symptomatic of a much larger problem: mindless consumerism combined with no specific financial goals. I don't encourage anyone to obsess over small purchases like a granola bar here or a smoothie there. I do encourage you to be radically real with yourself, though. Is it only here and there? Or, is it everywhere?

In my case, it was everywhere! I was making seemingly small purchases multiple times throughout the day. Then, on weekends I spent on slightly bigger purchases. This stuff added up substantially by the end of the month! It might not have been such a big deal if I had been a high-income earner, but I wasn't! My annual salary was $40,000, and I owed half that amount in credit card debt. There's no other word for this but *problem*!

Even after reading my first money book and going through my finances in detail, it took me a while to change my behavior. It wasn't until I had an "I can't take this anymore" moment that I got serious about my money. I was in the habit of stopping by the store to get a snack for my train ride home after work. A few days after going through all my statements, I realized I was eating snacks on the train when I already had snacks at home, less than thirty minutes away. There was no need for me to spend money on extra snacks, especially when I was trying to pay off my credit card debt. I knew I was going to have to cut myself off.

When I got home, I put my debit card and credit card away in my closet and packed only my MetroCard, lunch, and laptop for work the next day. After leaving my job the following day, I walked right into CVS and picked up snacks and a few other random items. I forgot I had no debit card or credit card in my bag. I was too embarrassed to tell the salesclerk I didn't have any money, so I told her I left my wallet in the car. What car? I was lying through my teeth! I never went back for that stuff, and I realized in that moment that the key to financial success is behavior, not knowledge.

I knew I had a spending problem. I knew I had $20,000 of credit card debt to pay off. I knew the snacks were unnecessary. None of that made it any easier to change my behavior. That was the wakeup call I needed. Let this be yours. Think about your spending habits. What are your budget leaks? Are any becoming a problem? What can you do to regain control?

Once I admitted I had a problem, I was ready to look for solutions. I wish I could say I cut back on all the unnecessary stuff overnight and squeezed discretionary income out of my budget like it was the last bit of toothpaste left in the tube! But it wasn't that simple. It helped that I stopped carrying money with me when I stepped outside each day. To this very day, I suggest people stay away from any technology features that make it easy for you to spend money in seconds without thinking it through. That's right—no Apple Pay! No digital wallets, and no memorizing your credit card details or storing them on every website where you shop.

Changing your spending behavior is challenging, but you can make it easier by creating friction the next time you spend. This doesn't have to be a permanent thing. It wasn't for me! Once I developed the self-control and knew I could trust myself not to spend mindlessly or out of boredom, I put the cards back in my wallet and activated "tap to pay." Figure out what you need to do to transition, but know that spending less is only one part of the action plan. Earning more is just as important.

Once I completed my master's program, I had more free time to generate extra income. I made a list of all my skills and credentials, and knew immediately that education was a field in which I could make good money on the side. I tutored on weekends. I became an onscreen instructor for a company that offered virtual courses to students falling behind in high school. I babysat as much as possible, and whenever the kids were napping or sleeping, I edited my YouTube videos.

When friends asked me to hang out, I was too embarrassed to say, "I don't have the money," so instead I hit them with, "Oh shoot, I'm busy. I blocked off that time to film videos for my YouTube channel."

To be real, I didn't consider that I could (or would) make money from my YouTube channel. I thought YouTubers got paid only if they got sponsorship deals. But after a year, I was getting checks from Google! Every time people saw banner ads while watching my videos, I was paid for it. This started off light, at about $100 per month, but eventually grew to thousands.

Then, people wanted to hire me to do speaking engagements, write guest blog posts, and make customized videos. It got to the point where friends would ask me to hang out and I legitimately had to pass because I was booked and busy, honey. Ultimately, the amazing team at Next Gen Personal Finance found my YouTube channel, and that led me to an even better and more aligned full-time job. The moral of the story is you shouldn't have to choose between cutting costs and making more. There's room for nuance, and you can do both!

BEYOND BUDGETING

The anti-budget helped me create data-driven roadblocks that prevent me from overspending. Digging into your spending data like the big tech companies do, and using that information to create simple structures for spending, is how to take control of your spending habits. But as someone who not only witnessed but also experienced the strain of being paid low wages, I know firsthand that many financial hardships can't be solved by budgeting.

Political decisions play a role in personal finance. To pretend they don't is to pretend government and workplace policies don't affect us daily as individuals. We need to be relentless in advocating for political and work-based initiatives that uplift struggling individuals and families, such as expanding family and medical leave, and the child tax credit. We need to vote for elected officials who fight to ensure minimum wage is enough to cover basic necessities like food, housing, transportation, and healthcare.

We need to demand that lawmakers and state education departments include a minimum of one semester of personal finance instruction for high school graduation requirements. For a list of states where high school personal finance is already required, as well as what you can do right now to help advocate in states where it's not yet required, download your free guide at mindyourmoneybook.com.

I'll forever empower historically underserved communities with financial education, but I'll never turn a blind eye to structural shortcomings. Achieving long-term, systemic changes in education laws, banking practices, and data privacy won't happen overnight. These are incredibly difficult and time-consuming commitments as it is, but they're even more challenging for those who have little money! While saving, budgeting, and leveraging credit will put you on a path to financial stability, they won't lead to any meaningful wealth accumulation. That's what investments are for!

CHAPTER 7

Investing: Set It and Forget It

I USED TO THINK INVESTING WAS LIKE THOSE DRAMATIC movie scenes where all the sweaty Wall Street guys in ties scream at their phones and computers as the clock ticks closer to the end of the day. Then I learned those aren't stock market investors—they're stock *traders*. It made me wonder who has that kind of time? I know it ain't me!

Researching companies in which to invest money is not a quick item on your to-do list. It takes time to read and analyze earnings reports, and then monitor individual stocks after buying them. I'm over here balancing work, family, my relationship, friends, self-care, and all the things! I don't know your life, but for me it feels like a constant juggling act to keep up.

Study after study proves that buying individual stocks is a losing strategy.[51] Your chance of making more money that

---

51 William F. Sharpe, "The Arithmetic of Active Management," *Financial Analysts Journal* 47, no. 1 (1991): 7–9, https://doi.org/10.2469/faj.v47.n1.7; J. B. Heaton, Nick Polson, and Jan Witte, "Why Indexing Works," *Applied Stochastic Models in Business and Industry* 33, no. 6 (2015): 690–93, http://dx.doi.org/10.2139/ssrn.2673262.

way is so slim, so why even waste your precious time and effort? I'm glad the data proves picking stocks doesn't work because I have zero interest in all that stock-picking mess. I'd rather spend time with my family and friends than obsess over stock charts.

Learning about investing feels like one big vocabulary test, so get ready to see a lot of new words. Learning the vocabulary helps demystify investing so it doesn't feel scary or intimidating. This chapter focuses on playing the long game by purchasing and holding shares of investment funds instead of individual stocks or bonds. I emphasize investing in exchange-traded funds and index funds, because that's what I invest in—and the data proves it works. Before we get to all the long-term investing gems, you first need a solid understanding of how the stock market works in general.

STOCK MARKETS AND SUPERMARKETS

Most of us have go-to brands or products we repeatedly buy. For me, it's Native deodorant, Clorox wipes, and Cholula hot sauce. When I'm running errands, I go into auto-pilot mode, rarely grabbing something different off the shelf. If I see my favorite products on sale, I almost always buy them in bulk. It feels like a no-brainer when the items are discounted—two or three for the price of one! That's at least 50 percent off the price I paid for the same exact products on my last trip to the supermarket.

Why wouldn't I stock up on products and save money? Our human brains love a good sale, so I know I'm not alone. Annual sales, clearance racks, BOGO. Yes, yes, and yes!

So, why is it that when the exact same thing happens

in the stock market instead of the supermarket, everybody freaks out. When stock prices for major American companies drop, every newspaper headline announces a stock market crash and people run in fear. *A recession is coming! A bear market is here! Another depression—run!*

Influencers on YouTube and TikTok post videos about the stock market, adding to the hype-machine and sometimes leading to full-on panic. This results in the least experienced and most fearful investors logging into their accounts and selling their stocks at these new, lower prices in an effort to hang on to whatever amount is still in their accounts. That's the worst thing to do because now these investors have locked in the losses by cashing out. *Yikes!*

It doesn't end there. After cashing out, they run and tell everybody they know about being burned in the stock market. Those who've never invested before feel scared, leading to more people saying, "Nope! I'm not putting my money in the stock market, because I'll lose it all in a crash." My reaction to this is the face-palm emoji. This is the equivalent of walking into the supermarket, noticing a storewide sale, and running out the door while yelling, "Oh no! Everything's on sale—this is terrible!" It makes no sense, right?

When the share price of a company's stock drops, think of it as a sale at the supermarket. Yesterday, people paid full price for this item, and today it's on sale! The most successful investors buy more shares when the market drops. They take advantage of the sale, just like they would in the supermarket.

Never before have we had direct and immediate access to income-producing assets, like stocks and bonds, regardless of who we are or where we come from. Every single one of the 94 percent of Americans who have access to broadband internet can directly access stock market investments from a computer or phone.[52] But as of 2022, only 58 percent have an investment account with stocks in it.[53] Why do you think that is?

At the start of my investing courses, I ask attendees to share their biggest hurdles to getting started investing. These are consistently the top three answers: lack of knowledge or education, lack of money to invest, and fear of losing money.

First off, if you're afraid to lose money investing, then you're operating 100 percent from a scarcity mindset—and we already know she ain't cute. Second, any American with an internet connection can start investing with as little as $1. Lack of money is no longer a barrier! Last, you do not need to become an investing pro. You only need to understand the basics to begin investing with confidence.

If you can learn the rules of Monopoly, you can learn to invest!

BORING, BUT POWERFUL

A 2017 paper proved that from 1926 to 2016 (ninety years), all the wealth creation in the stock market came from just 4 percent of stocks. The other 96 percent had returns matching the low interest you get on government bonds! In other words, the largest returns in the market come from very few stocks.[54] That small group of stocks is not the same every

52 "Eighth Broadband Progress Report," Federal Communications Commission, accessed March 5, 2023, https://www.fcc.gov/reports-research/reports/broadband-progress-reports/eighth-broadband-progress-report.

53 Lydia Saad and Jeffrey M. Jones, "What Percentage of Americans Own Stock?," *The Short Answer* (blog), Gallup, May 12, 2022, https://news.gallup.com/poll/266807/percentage-americans-owns-stock.aspx.

54 Hendrik Bessembinder, "Do Stocks Outperform Treasury Bills?," *Journal of Financial Economics* 129, no. 3 (September 2018): 440–57, https://doi.org/10.1016/j.jfineco.2018.06.004.

year, because if it were, we would all just invest in those and call it a day. Oh no, it's not that easy! Stocks represent ownership of a tiny portion of a publicly traded company's total value. The companies that come out on top each year are successful based on their performance, and that changes from year to year.

What makes anyone think they'll be lucky enough, year after year, to handpick those few winning companies from the thousands that exist? Greed—that's what! Greed, over-confidence, or desperation. This makes sense because we establish back in Chapter 2 that emotions drive people to make irrational moves.

Big tech companies go out of their way to collect data about us because they know the value of data-driven decisions. But if you're someone who doesn't care to learn all the nitty-gritty data and details about why passive investing works, there's a shortcut. It's not what you might expect. The most sensible, long-term, data-driven investing strategy based on more than one hundred years of stock market performance is the most boring of all.

It's boring, but powerful. So, listen up! I wish I could go back in time and share these words with my teenage self: open a brokerage account, buy as many shares of a low-cost, diversified exchange-traded fund (ETF) or index fund as you can afford every month, and keep doing this for decades.

Then again, Past Me would've had no clue what these words even mean. If you don't know either, keep reading because I break it down for you.

ASSETS OVER EVERYTHING

Throughout my childhood I heard family members mention

dreams of owning a plot of land in the Dominican Republic or a big house for our family to stay whenever we visited. It was as if the only forms of ownership we could envision were physical assets we could see and touch like real estate, farmland, a physical business, cars, or gold.

After some conversations about this with my friends, I realized most of them share this same experience. Many immigrants, like my parents, grew up in countries where banks are known for being weak or corrupt. They arrived in the United States with little to no understanding of how to navigate new institutions, financial products, and stock markets. In Chapter 3, we got into the rise and fall of the first bank for Black Americans, Freedman's Savings Bank. The tragic and corrupt events surrounding that bank's failure have had long-lasting repercussions. One is a lack of consumer trust in financial institutions, and another is a preference for tangible assets that can be seen and touched.

We also know technology has advanced tremendously over the centuries; wealth building is now more accessible than ever before. If we limit ourselves to only tangible assets, we'll never benefit from the countless intangible assets and financial assets that have historically yielded much greater returns for investors.

An asset is anything you own that has value and can be exchanged for cash. There are three types of assets you need to know about:

1. Real assets, also called tangible assets, usually come in physical form and get their value from their physical characteristics. These include gold, oil, land, real estate, physical businesses, and cars or other machinery.
2. Financial assets get their value from your ability to claim

ownership of something that may or may not be physical. This includes stocks, bonds, mutual funds, exchange-traded funds, investment accounts, bank deposits, and good old-fashioned cash.

3. Finally, there are intangible assets, which are strictly not physical. These include patents, copyrights, trademarks, intellectual property, and brand recognition.

The most successful and wealthy individuals tend to own all three types of assets, and you can too, even if you aren't all that wealthy yet! It pains me to see my community members put such a strong preference on assets they can see and touch, while they skip out on opportunities to invest in financial and intangible assets. That's the reason I dedicate this final chapter to investing in the stock market. I won't dig into real estate or other tangible assets, because they tend to be overhyped in communities of color. Tangible assets take much longer to sell and have higher transaction costs. They also often require additional related costs, such as insurance to keep them protected.

Worst of all, there are usually people, such as mortgage professionals, loan officers, and sales agents, who are involved in deciding whether or not you get to own these assets. This leaves room for people to discriminate and act as gatekeepers. Stock markets can't do that! When it comes to the stock market, you can invest in many asset classes, but we focus on two of the major ones: stocks and bonds.

WHAT'S A STOCK?

Stocks are called "equity" because they represent ownership in a company. This is the same concept as home equity, which represents the ownership someone has in their home. Let's say you and I bought a house and split the cost evenly. Neither of us owns the property outright, but we each own one out of two shares, or 50 percent equity. As the total value of this house increases over time, the value of each share also increases. For example, if the price of the house was $200,000 when we bought it, and it increased to $300,000 after a few years, our shares have gone from $100,000 each to $150,000 each in value. Keep in mind, we still each have a 50 percent share of ownership.

The same is true for the stock market, except instead of a house, you can own one or more shares of equity in a publicly traded company. That's why investors who buy stocks are called "shareholders." When the total value of a company increases, so does the value of each share of its stock. The main difference is that big companies don't have only two shares of ownership worth 50 percent each; they have tens of millions or *billions* of shares, which are referred to as "shares outstanding."

Buying a share of stock in a company gives you ownership of a tiny percentage of that company's total value. The number of shares outstanding gives you an idea of how many equal parts the company has been divided into. For example, Nike had 1.56 billion shares outstanding in the second week of November 2022, and each share's cost was about $106. Buying Nike stock for $106 would've gotten you one of 1.56 billion shares of ownership. Like I said, a tiny percentage of ownership, but hey, at least you're an owner and not just a consumer!

To make it easy for investors to buy, sell, and research stocks, each company assigns a "ticker symbol" to its stock. The symbol is a string of letters to form a code that looks similar to the company's name. Nike's ticker symbol is *NKE*, and Apple's is *AAPL*.

MARKET CAP

Public companies are categorized based on their total value, which is called "market capitalization," or "market cap" for short. This is just a fancy way of saying "the size of the company measured in dollars." How do investors calculate the market cap of a company? The same way they would for a house!

If you and I share our house equally and each share is worth $150,000, we multiply the total number of shares (two) by the price of each share ($150,000) for a total value of $300,000. When it comes to stocks, you share ownership with millions or billions of other investors, so you calculate the total value of the company by multiplying the number of shares outstanding by the price per share.

Let's go back to the second week of November 2022, when a share of Nike stock was valued at about $106. Since 1.56 billion shares were outstanding, we can easily calculate the company's total market cap at that time. Simple multiplication (1.56 billion shares outstanding x $106 per share) shows the market cap was roughly $165,300,000,000.

Companies that have a market cap above $10 billion are considered "large-cap" companies, while those between $2 billion and $10 billion are called "mid-cap" companies. When a company's market cap is below $2 billion, it's called a "small-cap" company.

These categories are directly linked to the amount of risk investors take when investing. In the world of investing, "risk" means your chances of losing money on an investment. If an investor is willing to take on more risk by investing in smaller companies that lack the resources of larger companies, they invest in small-cap stocks. These stocks are less stable than large-cap ones, meaning they're more likely to fail. However, those that end up doing well experience major growth because they have a lot of room to reach mid-cap or large-cap status.

Large-cap stocks are from companies that are already very big, and they tend to have a stronger reputation with consumers. The chances of these companies going broke overnight are slim, so they're less likely to fail. They provide stability for investors and are more mature than smaller companies in the market.

Mid-cap stocks are right in between, with a medium level of risk and stability. They offer potential for growth, but with less risk than small-cap stocks.

BEAR VERSUS BULL

When the stock market drops (specifically by a decrease of at least 20 percent from its previous high), it's called a "bear market." Between 1957 and 2018, the average length of a bear market was just under a year, which is very short.[55] When the stock market goes up, specifically by an increase of at least 20 percent from its previous low, it's called a "bull market." In the same sixty-one-year period from 1957 to 2018, the average length of a bull market was four and a half years. Nice!

Not only do the good times last about five times longer on average compared to the bad, but they also happen way

---

55 "Bull and Bear Markets—Historical Trends and Portfolio Impact," Invesco, accessed March 5, 2023, https://retirecertain.com/wp-content/uploads/2019/10/how-to-prepare-for-bear-markets-chart-1024x764.png.

more often! Looking at the stock market year by year for the ninety-one years ending in 2018, you'll notice the market was up about 75 percent of the time and down about 25 percent of the time. It's a fact that bad times will come. Downturns, recessions, market crashes, and bear markets will definitely happen. We just don't know when they'll come or how long they'll linger.

So, we need to be prepared for bad times to strike at any time. Every investor needs to have an emergency savings fund stacked with cash and a clear investing plan. As an investor, you must know how much time you plan to keep your money in the market. This is your "time horizon."

If you're investing for your baby niece's college tuition and they just turned three, you have a fifteen-year time horizon for investing. We know this because in fifteen years that niece will turn eighteen and be ready for college. That's plenty of time for the stock market to go up and down. That's called "market volatility," and it's a normal part of the investing process. With a fifteen-year time horizon, you can afford to take more risk than investors whose kids are already in high school.

If I have a goal of retiring in five years, I'll have a much shorter time horizon and much lower tolerance for risk compared to you and your niece. That's because five years is one-third of the fifteen-year time horizon you have. To retire, I'd need a large sum of money in my investment account, so I don't want to risk losing money in the market when I'm just five years away. If a bear market suddenly hits in my five-year window, I'd see my account balance drop by a lot! I wouldn't have enough money to retire as planned, and I'd probably need to keep working until the market recovers. Who knows how long that would take?

Although the historical average length of a bear market is less than a year, we have no way of predicting how long each specific bear market will last once it hits.[56] It could be much shorter or much longer than the average.

The level of risk an investor takes is based on how much time they have left before they need to start withdrawing money for their financial goal. The more time you have, the more risk you can tolerate. More risk in your portfolio means you have more stocks and fewer bonds. That also means you have more potential for profits. Investors use time horizon to decide the right mix of stocks versus bonds for them. Mostly stocks and a little bit of bonds? Or all stocks? When you're super close to retiring, you don't want to have all stocks in your portfolio—that's way too risky.

Any investor who's completely uncomfortable with the thought of their account balance dropping, even temporarily, should not invest in stocks at all until they become familiar with lessons from historical data. Until then, they're better off investing in bonds, which are less risky than stocks, and come with lower returns on average as a result. No risk, no potential reward.

WHAT'S A BOND?

When you invest in bonds, you're a "bondholder" and you become a lender, not an owner. Bonds represent money you've lent to a company or to the government. Basically, they owe you the money you lent to them, plus interest on top. If you invest in a corporate bond, you're lending your money to a corporation that issued a bond—the "bond issuer." If you

---

56   Hartford Funds, "10 Things You Should Know about Bear Markets," Client Conversations, accessed March 5, 2023, https://www.hartfordfunds.com/dam/en/docs/pub/whitepapers/CCWP045.pdf.

choose to invest in a municipal bond, you're lending money to a city or local government agency. There are also Treasury bonds, or T-bonds for short, which means you're lending your money to the federal government of the United States.

Why would anyone want to lend their money to corporations or to the government?

Remember how we talked about banks and credit unions giving us interest when we put money in their savings accounts? Well, becoming a bondholder means you're the one collecting interest payments since you do the lending. Since the interest you collect from a bond doesn't change, bonds are referred to as "fixed income" investments.

Stocks (a.k.a. equities) constantly go up and down like a roller coaster, and that volatility makes it hard to predict what might happen to your account balance in the short term. Bonds offer a fixed interest rate, called a "coupon rate." They also have a set payment schedule for your coupon payments to hit your account—typically, every six months. This makes it easy for bondholders to predict how much they'll see in their account and when. Bonds are low-risk investments, but high in stability and predictability. That's best for investors who don't have a lot of time left to invest before they need to take money out of their investment account. They have a short time horizon. (Think retirees or anyone approaching the event they're investing for, such as parents looking to withdraw money from a college savings plan for their child to start college in a few years.)

Bonds give you a chance to make more money than you would in a traditional savings account, but not as much as you would in the stock market. Remember, the lower the risk, the lower the potential reward!

The fixed interest rate in a savings account is guaranteed

by the bank if it's an FDIC-insured account (or NCUA-insured for credit unions). That means your money is protected and backed by the government—up to $250,000 per account. This is the kind of safety and security we need for emergency fund money, and that's why we keep that in a high-yield savings account. However, even a high-yield savings account will never earn more than the fixed interest rate offered by banks or credit unions—which is generally low. That's why wealth building does not happen in a savings account.

ASSET ALLOCATION

If I want to retire in five years or less, a majority of my portfolio should be allocated to bonds, not to stocks. If the stock market crashes, it won't affect my account too much because I bought more bonds and less stocks over time. The further you are from your goal, the riskier you can be. That means you have mostly stock investments, and you shift to bonds slowly over time so that when you retire your portfolio will be mostly made up of bonds and only a small percentage of stocks. This prevents the bulk of your money from being exposed to the full risk and volatility of the stock market.

Most financial experts say that when it comes to your retirement portfolio, you should take the difference of the number 125 minus your age and use that figure as the percentage of stocks for your portfolio. For a twenty-five-year-old (or younger), 125 minus 25 is 100 percent of their retirement portfolio allocated to stocks. For a sixty-five-year-old, 125 minus 65 is 60 percent of their portfolio invested in stocks. That makes sense because they're forty years older than a twenty-five-year-old and have a much lower time horizon for retirement.

This process of figuring out the right mix between stocks and bonds is called "asset allocation." It's important that every few years, as you get closer to your financial goal and your time horizon gets shorter, you reallocate your portfolio. You can use the 125 minus your age rule as a starting point, but you can always adjust from there and choose to be more risky or aggressive, or more conservative. You've got to make sure you're still on track to have a healthy mix of stocks versus bonds, and that the mix you have at any given point isn't too risky or overly safe.

If you're willing to pay a little more each year to have this process automated in your retirement portfolio, consider buying target date funds. The target date is the year you expect or plan to retire, and as that year approaches the fund automatically sells stocks to buy more bonds. We talk more about investment funds later in this chapter.

THE RULE OF 72

The average interest rate for a savings account has been close to zero percent since the Great Recession in 2008. Ouch! There's a cute and easy math formula called the Rule of 72, which shows you the long-term effect of interest rates on your money. If you know what interest rate you're getting, you can find out how long it will take you to double your money at that rate. To use this rule, divide 72 by the interest rate, and the answer provides the number of years it'll take to double your money. For example, let's say you put $100 into a savings account at a 2 percent rate. Divide 72 by 2, and you'll see it'll take thirty-six years for that $100 to double and become $200. Yep, thirty-six years!

The historical average interest rate on US government

bonds is about 5 percent, while the average return of the five hundred leading companies in the U.S. stock market is about 10 percent.[57] Using the Rule of 72, we know it would take 14.4 years to double our money with bonds, while it would take only 7.2 years to double it with stocks. That's half as much time, and it makes a huge difference!

The Rule of 72 works whenever you're dealing with amounts that grow exponentially over time. This is called "compounding," which Albert Einstein called the "eighth wonder of the world" for a reason. But there's a big difference between compounding interest and compounding returns.

COMPOUND INTEREST VERSUS COMPOUND RETURNS

I've never read a better explanation about the difference between interest and returns than the one posted on Ellevest in 2021. The post shares a great example of how compound interest works. Here's a quote:

> For example, if a savings account pays the current national average of about 1%, then your money will increase by 1% every year... But compounding can work against you, too—like when you owe compound interest on debt. For example, if the annual interest rate on your credit card is the current national average of about 18%, then the amount of debt you owe will increase by 18% every year.[58]

57 Aswath Damodaran, "Historical Returns on Stocks, Bonds and Bills: 1928–2022," NYU Stern School of Business, January 2023, https://pages.stern.nyu.edu/~adamodar/New_Home_Page/datafile/histretSP.html.

58 Ellevest Team, "The 'Magic' of Compounding, Explained," *Ellevest Magazine*, March 9, 2021, https://www.ellevest.com/magazine/investing/compounding-returns.

Ouch! That's exactly what happened to me with those credit cards back in college. Let's look at what the article says about compound returns:

> Compound returns usually come up when we talk about investing. In this case, you aren't earning *interest*, which is a promised, steady amount—you're potentially earning *investing returns*, which are definitely not guaranteed and definitely not steady. But they can be super powerful...
>
> When the value of the individual investments you own, like stocks and bonds, goes up (or down), that makes the balance in your investment account go up (or down). As long as you leave the difference invested, then your returns have the opportunity to compound over time.
>
> So if the markets were to go up for a big chunk of the time you had money invested, compounding would work in your favor. And yes, that goes the other way too if the markets decline— that's why we say that investing comes with risk. BUT. The longer you let compounding work its mathemagic, the more likely you are to have overall positive returns (at least, that's been the case historically). Case in point: Stocks are typically the riskiest part of an investment portfolio, and they've gone up in about 75% of years since 1928—in fact, the stock market's average annual return has been about 9.6%.
>
> *That's* why investing can be more useful than simply saving as you work toward your money goals, build wealth, and take advantage of the market's potential for growth.
>
> So getting started ASAP is a big deal—the higher your account's

balance and the longer your money's invested, the more opportunity it has to compound over time.

Every day you wait is a day you miss out on the opportunity to start compounding.[59]

I told you it's the best explanation! Mathemagic is officially my new favorite word. The Ellevest team did that. I love this post so much because one of my nerdy pet peeves is when people say you get compound interest in the stock market. No, you don't! You get compound *returns* in the stock market.

In case you're wondering why people confuse these terms or use them interchangeably on purpose, it's because the mathematical formula for compounding is the same in both cases. We all call it the "compound interest formula," even though technically it's the compounding formula. We use the label "compound interest calculator" when we should say "compounding calculator."

The math is the same for compounding returns, compounding interest, and compounding fees. Compounding is compounding! Since the math is the same, people just assume the language is the same, too. Not you, though! You know there's an important difference between compound interest and compound returns.

Maybe you're thinking, *Forget that compound interest mess! It takes too long to double my money. I'm just gonna invest in the stock market and get those higher compound return rates so I can double all my money faster!* Hold on now. Slow your roll.

In Chapter 3, we established that you need to set aside

---

59   Ellevest Team, "The 'Magic' of Compounding."

your emergency fund, preferably in a high-yield savings account. Since there's no risk of losing money in your FDIC-insured savings account, you can count on that money being there when you need it. That's not the case with investments! You should only invest *after* you've set up your emergency fund and reached your savings goal.

Banks and credit unions are great places to save for your short-term goals, but when it comes to big #moneygoals— paying for college, buying a house, retiring with dignity—the stock market is where it's at! Investing is for building wealth, and that takes decades, not days. Imagine trying to get six-pack abs overnight. Ha! Good luck with that one.

Okay, I know you get it. Investing is for building real wealth over the long term. *This ain't a get-rich-quick scheme.* How do you make sure you don't lose money over the years, though? Well, you can't. When it comes to investing, there's no way to completely eliminate risk. All you can do is lower your risk, and you do this by diversifying your investments.

DIVERSIFICATION

The classic phrase people use to explain diversification is this: *don't put all your eggs in one basket.* They always forget to add the next part, which is really important: *don't put all your eggs in one basket because if you should drop the basket, you lose all your eggs.* When it comes to investing, it translates to this: *don't put all your money into one stock because if that stock drops to zero, you lose all your money.*

There are about four thousand companies issuing stock in the United States alone! The people picking individual stocks try to guess which will be the best-performing with the highest returns. There's no way of knowing which will perform the best unless you have a crystal ball and can see the future. If you have those powers, email me right away to missbehelpful@gmail.com and let me know!

Even if you buy four hundred stocks you think are the best and have them all in your portfolio, that's only 10 percent of all the companies in America! You could be missing the real winners among the other 90 percent because stocks all have the potential to grow in value. The chances of one company failing are very high. But the chances of hundreds or thousands of companies all failing at the same time are slim to none.

The only way to completely minimize the risk of missing out on the best-performing companies is to invest in them all because the larger the number of stocks in your portfolio, the lower the risk you take. The reverse is also true. The smaller the number of stocks in your portfolio, the more risk you take. *So, you're saying we should all buy hundreds or thousands of stocks? Wouldn't that be expensive? Doesn't that take hours and hours? How would we even know which ones to buy?*

Okay, *cálmate*. Calm down. That's where investment funds come in!

Would you rather go to the store every day to buy an individual roll of toilet paper or would you rather buy a jumbo pack of thirty-six rolls in one trip to the store? Just think of how every time you run out of TP, you'd have to go back to the store to buy another roll. That's ridiculous! Nobody wants to do that. I much prefer to buy a bundle, especially if it's on sale! With one purchase, I get dozens of toilet paper rolls at once.

That's the idea behind investment funds. They're bundles of stocks, bonds, or a mix of both, which you can buy in bulk to make your investment life easier! The two main types of investment funds you need to know about are mutual funds and exchange-traded funds.

MUTUAL FUNDS VERSUS ETFS

Mutual funds and exchange-traded funds (ETFs) are bundles of hundreds or thousands of stocks, bonds, or a mix of both. That means they're automatically diversified. However, these two types of investment funds operate completely differently.

Mutual funds can be bought or sold only once per trading day. Regular stock market trading day hours are from 9:30 a.m. ET to 4:00 p.m. ET. When you buy or sell shares of a mutual fund, the exact price of that transaction isn't revealed until the end of the trading day. This is a limitation mutual funds have because they're old-school investments. They were created in the 1920s, and became popular in the 1970s and '80s.

ETFs are the cooler, younger cousin. ETFs were created in 1993, so they're more modern. Unlike mutual funds, they can be bought and sold by investors throughout the trading day. In other words, these investment funds can be traded on a stock market exchange in real time (the same way individual stocks can) but they hold hundreds or thousands of stocks. That's why they got the name "exchange-traded funds." They're funds that can be traded on an exchange. Those old-school mutual funds can't do that!

Mutual funds and ETFs are investment funds that both offer many different stocks, bonds, or a mix of both. They're less risky than buying individual stocks, because they're automatically diversified. A mutual fund that holds only stocks is called an "equity fund." ETFs that hold only stocks are called "equity ETFs." Mutual funds that hold only bonds are called "bond funds," or "fixed income funds." ETFs that hold only bonds are called "bond ETFs," or "fixed income ETFs."

There are even mutual funds that have a mix of stocks and bonds inside! Those are called "balanced funds." For those who prefer ETFs, you can buy "balanced ETFs" instead. There's a flavor for every taste! Mutual funds and ETFs have different rules about how and when they can be traded, and they're also different when it comes to the costs. Let's start with mutual fund costs.

All investment funds have an annual fee for management and marketing, called an "expense ratio." This annual fee is shown as a percentage, just like the interest on your savings account. The difference is that you're paying this rate, not collecting it! Your goal should be to pay the lowest fees possible so you can keep more of your hard-earned money and compound gains in the market over time.

You already know the world of investing is just a long vocabulary test. Once you learn the terminology, nobody can talk to you like you're an outsider or make you feel dumb. You'll know your stuff, honey. Knowledge is power, and no one can ever take away what you know once you know it! If you're going to pick mutual funds, index funds, or ETFs for your own investment accounts, then the "expense ratio" is one of the most important terms to know!

If you have $100 in a savings account and you get 1 percent in interest, your account balance goes up to $101 at the end of the year. This is also how the expense ratio of an investment fund works, but it gets subtracted. If you have $100 invested and your expense ratio is 1 percent, your account balance drops to $99 after a year. Now, this might not sound like a big deal, but two things of note make it a bigger deal.

First, these investing costs compound just like your

returns do. Second, the fees are charged on all "assets under management," or AUM. So as your account balance grows from your earnings and profits, you get charged a fee on the growing account balance. This means you pay fees on the dollars you deposit, plus the profits you earn. It also means you pay more in fees as your account balance grows and compounds.

We already know mutual funds are old-school, but the super-duper old-school ones are called "traditional mutual funds," which are actively managed. That means they have a mutual fund manager responsible for picking the stocks or bonds they think will make the most returns for the investors of that fund. They're called "active managers," because they do all the active work of researching, analyzing, buying and selling stocks, and monitoring the fund over time. That means investors don't have to do any of this work themselves!

This might look great at first...but once you see how much the costs and fees eat away at your compound returns, you'll feel differently! When a fund comes with an active manager, it also comes with a much higher expense ratio. For example, let's say you got $100,000 from an accident settlement or inheritance, and you want to invest it all at once and not add any more money for twenty years. Using a compounding calculator and assuming a 10 percent average return rate, you'll find this money would grow to $672,750.

But, that's not including any fees. Now, let's say everything about the scenario stays the same, except now you have an expense ratio of 1 percent on your fund. That 1 percent annual fee comes out of your average annual returns. Instead of a 10 percent average return, you're now down to a 9 percent average return after subtracting the fee. Okay, let's do this again with $100,000 invested—not a penny more—a twenty-year time horizon, and a 9 percent rate of return. The compounding calculator says… Drum roll, please! The grand total is $560,441.

Um, that's $112,309 less, meaning you paid $112,309 in fees for that active management approach. *Ouch!*

What if you were to invest that same $100,000 for twenty years, but this time with an expense ratio that's ten times cheaper? Instead of paying 1 percent, you pay 0.1 percent. That comes right out of your expected returns, so your 10 percent average return drops to 9.9 percent. What happens then? Let's pull up that compounding calculator and run it back!

Well, will you look at that! A whole $660,623. You pay a total of $12,127 in fees instead of paying $112,309. *Wow, wow, wow!*

Famous investor John Bogle (may he rest in peace) said, "We have the miracle of compounding returns overwhelmed by the tyranny of compounding costs." He used the word "tyranny," which means "cruel and oppressive." *Whew!* That tells us what we need to know. Be careful with the costs and fees associated with active investing.

Many financial professionals who charge you for investing advice or active management of funds might make it seem like a 1 percent expense ratio is not too bad. A lot of people agree and say it's not that big of a deal. Not you, though! You know that over a twenty-, thirty-, or forty-year wealth-building journey, a 1 percent annual fee will compound and seriously eat away at your returns. You know how important it is to avoid high expense ratios and other unnecessary fees, such as sales loads. Those are commission fees that add profits to the investment manager's pocket, not the pockets of investors.

INDEX FUNDS

That famous investor I mentioned, John Bogle, is the founder of Vanguard—a unique investment company that changed the game in 1976. Uncle Bogle could've created another typical for-profit publicly traded company that depends on higher management fees to make profits. Instead, he used a mutual ownership structure, which means Vanguard is owned by the investors in its funds. This benefits investors because any profits Vanguard earns are returned to investors in the form of lower fees. That's a really big deal!

Uncle Bogle and his team at Vanguard created a special type of mutual fund, called an "index fund." Instead of a costly active manager choosing the stocks held by the fund, index funds just invest in the stocks or bonds from a pre-created list, also called an index! The word "index" literally means "list," which is where the index fund gets its name.

Flip to the back of any textbook, and you'll typically find an index. That's a list of all the topics in the book and the page number for each topic. Index funds make investing super easy by copying investments from a list so you don't have to choose or pay someone hefty fees to make those choices for you. To make it onto these lists, companies must meet strict requirements. It's like a student making honor roll! Not just any student makes the honor roll, because it's based on academic performance. It's the same concept with an index!

You've probably already heard of some of the most famous index lists. Examples include the Standard and Poor's 500, or S&P 500—a list of five hundred leading large-cap American companies—and the Dow Jones Industrial Average, nicknamed "the Dow." The Dow was the first-ever index list of stocks, and it includes thirty leading, large-cap American companies. Note that a list of five hundred companies (S&P 500) is much more diversified than a list of thirty. Investing in a fund that copies or mirrors the Dow is riskier than investing in a fund that mimics the S&P 500.

Index funds cut the cost of investing in funds by ten times or greater! Actively managed mutual funds charge an expense ratio of 0.8 percent to 1 percent per year on average. Index funds cut these costs down to 0.04 percent to 0.1 percent per year on average. Investing $5,000 in an index fund costs you just $5 a year instead of $50 per year for an actively managed mutual fund with similar holdings.

Bogle basically said, *You know, all this expensive active research and analysis just doesn't make sense when we have so many pre-created lists to copy.* He realized that tremendously cutting fees saves everyday investors huge amounts of money over time. As you might imagine, this was really controversial in the investing industry at the time! It's like my dad angrily driving his old-school taxicab with no clients, while Uber and Lyft get all the business.

Disruption is often a byproduct of innovation and technology. Financial professionals who were used to making piles of money from active management were not happy that a cheaper alternative was created. It was a blow to the active management industry, but a win for investors. No longer would financial pros be able to line their pockets with the hard-earned money of the everyday investor. No longer could anyone claim that tiny-looking percentage-point differences in fees don't matter. No longer would people be able to make a case for paying high fees for actively managed mutual funds.

Whenever I teach people about index funds, someone always asks, "But what about the returns? Isn't there a case for paying more in fees if it will lead to better returns?" Well, that's easy. You *don't* get better returns!

There's research comparing actively managed mutual funds to their competing benchmark index. The results aren't even close! Over a ten-year period or longer, 90 percent of actively managed mutual funds do worse than index funds in the United States. That means they charge higher fees for worse results.[60] That's trash!

The most famous index, by far, is the S&P 500, and most brokerage firms have their own index fund that mirrors this index. For example, Vanguard 500 Index Fund Admiral Shares (ticker symbol VFIAX), Fidelity 500 Index Fund (ticker symbol FXAIX), and Schwab S&P 500 Index Fund (ticker symbol SWPPX) all hold the same stocks—the same ones listed on the S&P 500 index.

Index investing is a no-brainer for well-known American stocks like the ones in the S&P 500, because active managers can't get any special insights over the index list. You should never pay for active management of these types of investments.

We've established that index funds are a special type of mutual fund that doesn't come with an active manager and therefore cuts the fees ten times lower. So, what are the major differences between investing in an index fund versus an ETF if they both hold the same stocks or bonds? Well, remember ETFs can be traded throughout the day. If you buy an ETF at 9:30 a.m. ET, you can sell it at 9:31 a.m. ET. Some investors like this flexibility. If you're investing for the long term, like I am, then you don't care very much about that perk.

---

60 Spiva, "Spiva Data: Results by Region: U.S.," S&P Dow Jones Indices, accessed March 5, 2023, https://www.spglobal.com/spdji/en/research-insights/spiva/.

Another major difference is the amount you need to get started. With most mutual funds, investors can't just start with any amount they want. They need to buy at least the minimum amount required to start investing. That's usually a few thousand dollars, which ain't cheap! ETFs, on the other hand, require investors to buy only one share of the fund—usually hundreds of dollars, not thousands. This makes ETFs more affordable for investors looking to start investing without a lot of money.

With the rise of "fractional share investing" on most major platforms, you can even buy any dollar amount of an ETF share instead of paying the full share price. For example, let's say you have a budget of $100 to start investing and you want to buy Vanguard 500 Index Fund Admiral Shares (ticker symbol VFIAX). Since the minimum investment for that index fund is more than $1,000, it's out of your budget. So, you check out Vanguard 500 Index Fund ETF instead. It holds the same stocks but has the ticker symbol VOO. You notice the share price is $300. You can still buy $100 worth of VOO, and you'll own one-third of a share.

Fractional shares allow you to buy pricier ETFs and stocks for as little as $1. Investors with smaller budgets can buy and own companies that otherwise might be out of reach. Accessing the financial markets has never been easier! ETFs have quickly become popular, because not only are they low-cost, with the flexibility of real-time trading and history of strong performance, but they also tend to result in less taxes compared to mutual funds. This helps investors save even more money over time.

BUYING INVESTMENTS

Imagine going on vacation with no suitcase or carry-on bag. You just show up at the airport with all your belongings in your hands. I'm talking clothes, sneakers, toiletries, accessories, and more stacked in a big pile in your arms like laundry. The security and TSA agents would look at you as if you'd lost your mind. You need something to put your stuff in. Investments are like stuff—they need a container!

The first step to buying investments, such as stocks, bonds, mutual funds, index funds, or ETFs, is to open an investment account. These are also called "brokerage accounts," because you can open one at any brokerage firm or investment bank you choose. Some popular brokerages are Fidelity, Charles Schwab, Vanguard, E-Trade, and TD Ameritrade.

Opening an account with a brokerage is just like opening a bank account with a bank or credit union. Do some comparison shopping to find out who offers the best deals, the accounts you need, educational videos and articles, strong customer service, and an easy-to-use website or app. If you care about things like fractional share investing or access to international stock exchanges, look into those things, too.

Don't spend too much time deciding which brokerage to use, because you can always change it later. The important thing is to get started ASAP. Next, decide what type of account you want to open. This will depend on why you want to invest money. Most people begin investing because they don't want to work forever. They know that once they build up enough money to cover their monthly expenses for years and years, they can retire and stop working full time. (We talk in the next section about how much money it takes to retire.)

Investment accounts designed specifically for retirement

include 401(k), 403(b), and individual retirement accounts (IRAs). If your job offers you a retirement plan like a 401(k) or 403(b), that's the easiest way to invest for retirement! You just fill out some paperwork or complete an online form, and a small amount of money comes out of your paycheck before your income is taxed. It gets deposited into your retirement account and is used to buy shares of mutual funds or index funds, which you get to choose when you complete the paperwork to sign up.

Strongly consider signing up if your company offers a "401(k) match." If you put money into your 401(k), the company matches that up to a certain amount of dollars or up to a certain percentage of your salary. If your company has a 10 percent match per year, and you contribute 10 percent of your salary each year, the company matches that amount with extra money on top of your salary. That brings your 401(k) account balance up to 20 percent of your salary, even though you only put in 10 percent yourself. The match is free money from the company, and you should see it as part of your salary and benefits package. It's a savvy financial move in the long run if you get the full match in every 401(k) plan throughout your career.

If your job doesn't offer a retirement plan, open your own at a brokerage of your choice, as long as they offer individual retirement accounts (IRAs). We take a closer look at IRAs later in this chapter.

Some people invest for their children's education since college tuition is very expensive! Beginning to invest a small amount of money every week or month when the kids are still cute babies ensures that when they turn eighteen, they'll have almost two decades of compounding returns stacked up. That's way better than collecting compound interest in a savings account. The most popular investment account for education is a 529 plan. All fifty states have a 529 plan they sponsor. You can easily find yours by searching online for the name of your state and the term "529 plan."

There's even an investment account designed specifically for health and medical costs! It's called a health savings account (HSA). If you use your HSA to pay for qualified medical expenses, you don't pay taxes on that money. Notice it says "qualified" expenses, because not all medical costs qualify for these tax breaks. If all medical costs were qualified, people would go to the spa all the time and say it's a medical cost. Come on. Uncle Sam is smarter than that!

Each account I've mentioned has annual limits that prevent you from contributing more than a fixed dollar amount for any given year. They also come with strict rules about when you can access the money. If you take the money out too soon, you'll pay penalty fees and taxes!

If you're a baller looking to invest with no annual limits or a rebel who doesn't appreciate strict rules about when you can or can't touch your own money, consider a taxable investment account. This is also called a "taxable brokerage account" or "standard brokerage account." It's a very popular account for investors looking to grow wealth for reasons besides retirement, education, or health. Retirement plans and 529 plans typically have a list of pre-selected mutual funds and index funds to choose from, but taxable investment accounts do not! You get the freedom to choose any investments your heart desires.

I always say start with retirement accounts first to take care of Future You. Then, any extra money you might have can be invested outside of a retirement account by opening that taxable brokerage account. Starting with a retirement account is major, because you'll likely need to build up a really large amount of money before you can stop working full time.

WHEN CAN I RETIRE?

Well, that's not the right question. The real question is this: *How much money do I need to retire?*

Back in 1998, I was blasting Brandy and Monica's "The Boy is Mine," and I was not thinking about retirement. But three professors at Trinity University were! They released a study that calculated a safe amount of money anyone could withdraw from their investments during retirement without running out of money too soon. The dollar amount was different for everyone, depending on their spending, of course, but the study focused on a withdrawal rate. The professors figured out what percentage of your investments you can withdraw yearly to cover your living expenses when you're no longer working. That withdrawal rate is 4 percent.[61]

To stick to a 4 percent withdrawal rate, investors need to build up twenty-five times their annual expenses in their retirement account. For my fellow math nerds out there, the math on this is 25 × 4 percent = 100 percent.

This is called the 25x Rule, which is what a lot of early retirees in the FIRE (Financial Independence Retire Early) community use to plan for early retirement. If you expect to spend $5,000 a month in retirement, you'll need $60,000 per year ($5,000 × 12 months). That means you'll need to grow your investment account to be 25 × $60,000, or $1.5 million,

---

61   Philip L. Cooley, Carl M. Hubbard, and Daniel T. Walz, "Retirement Savings: Choosing a Withdrawal Rate That Is Sustainable," *AAII Journal* (February 1998): 16–21, https://www.aaii.com/journal/199802/feature.pdf.

in order to retire. Then, you can withdraw 4 percent of that, or $60,000, per year without running low on money.

Ready to use the 25x Rule for your financial planning? Think of how much money you'd like to spend each month in retirement, then multiply that by twelve months to find your annual spending amount. Multiply that number by twenty-five, and see what you get. Will you need $2 million, $3 million, or more? It can be scary to see a number so big, but don't worry—the stock market can help you!

BACKWARD PLAN

I look over my financial net worth a few times a year. Every time I do this, I pull up a compounding calculator and enter my starting amount of money, monthly or annual additions, and length of time in years before I want to retire. I set it to compound annually at the historical return rate of the S&P 500, or 10 percent. Then I look to see if the result is equal to or greater than my 25x number.

I surpassed the $100,000 mark in my 401(k) account in 2021. It was the first time I could envision myself retiring early. Using a compounding calculator, I entered an initial amount of $100,000 and a monthly contribution of $500. For length of time, I entered twenty years, and for average return rate, I selected 10 percent. The result was over $1 million. That might not seem like a lot of money to some people, but it meant a lot to me to see that I'm on track for a million with just $16 a day! I know a lot of retired individuals in my family and my community, and not very many of them have accumulated a million dollar financial net worth. Don't downplay that! It's a big deal.

I like to say that investing and taxes are like café con leche (coffee and milk). They go together, and you can't separate them. You can't jump into investing without understanding the tax implications. In the United States, you pay taxes on the profits your investments make but only when you sell them. So, if you own an investment and the price goes up, but you keep holding it, you don't have to pay taxes on it! The profits you make from selling investments are called "capital gains," and they get taxed anytime you sell investment assets like stocks, bonds, mutual funds, ETFs, precious metals, cryptocurrencies, and collectibles.

What you pay and when you need to pay depend on the type of investment account you have and a few other important factors. One of the most important factors is how long you held your investments. Holding investments longer than a year allows you to pay long-term capital gains tax, which is broken down by brackets of 0 percent, 15 percent, and 20 percent based on your taxable income. According to the IRS, the tax rate on most net capital gains is 15 percent for most individuals.[62]

Selling your investments in less than a year results in a short-term capital gains tax with a higher tax brackets ranging from 10 percent to 37 percent. These match up with ordinary income tax brackets, and that means you pay more when you sell investments too soon.

Another way investors are taxed is if they receive dividends, which are payments companies make to share their profits with shareholders. Dividends are generally taxable in the year they were received, even if you didn't sell them

---

62 "Topic No. 409 Capital Gains and Losses," Tax Topics, Internal Revenue Service, last modified January 26, 2023, https://www.irs.gov/taxtopics/tc409.

for cash. Dividend details get sent to you after the year ends on a 1099 DIV form so you can report it when you file your taxes. It can sound a bit complex when you're new to investing, but once you go through it for the first time, you'll see how easy it can be.

THE ROTH IRA IS THE G.O.A.T.

There are two types of capital gains: unrealized and realized. Unrealized gain refers to an increase in the value of an investment you hold that leads to an increase in your account balance. The key is that it has not been sold for cash yet. A realized gain is created when an investment is sold for cash and makes a profit.

The tax rate you pay on capital gains depends on whether they're short- or long-term capital gains. If you were to sell an investment at a profit between January 1 and December 31 of 2023, you'd need to report it when you file taxes by the April 2024 filing deadline. However, the rules are different when it comes to capital gains inside of an IRA!

IRAs have different tax rules because they're "tax sheltered," which means they allow investors to minimize the current or future taxes owed. The two main types of IRA accounts are the traditional IRA and the Roth IRA. To open either one of these accounts, you must have taxable income from wages, salaries, commissions, tips, bonuses, or net income from a business you operate. The only exception to this rule is if you are married and out of work or have very limited income, in which case you can open a Spousal IRA and contribute along with your spouse.

Realized gains in a Traditional IRA are tax-deferred, so you don't have to pay them until you withdraw money in retirement. Realized gains in a Roth IRA are *never taxed* as long as certain conditions are met. That's why I say that when it comes to investing accounts, the Roth IRA is the G.O.A.T. (greatest of all time). Let's get into more details for each type of IRA.

There are no income limits for opening a traditional IRA, so anyone can have one. Money you deposit in the account, called "contributions," can be partially or fully deducted from your taxable income when you file your taxes, lowering your tax obligation. The downside is that not every investor who contributes to a traditional IRA qualifies for this tax benefit. Income thresholds apply to high-income earners and employees who have a retirement plan through their job.

Most Americans, however, can use the traditional IRA to lower their tax bill for every year they contribute to this account. For example, if your taxable income is $16,500 and you bought $6,500 worth of ETFs inside your traditional IRA, you subtract the IRA contribution amount from your taxable income, bringing it down to $10,000.

After age fifty-nine and a half, you do have to pay taxes when you withdraw money from your traditional IRA. That means if your $6,500 contribution grew to $7,000, you wouldn't have to pay capital gains tax on that $500 profit until you withdraw the money in retirement. You need to be careful not to withdraw funds too soon, though. If you withdraw from a traditional IRA before turning fifty-nine and a half, you'll owe taxes and a 10 percent penalty unless you qualify for an early withdrawal exception. Those exceptions include a first-time home purchase, certain medical costs, and higher education costs.

The Roth IRA is the only investment account that lets you grow your money tax-free while allowing access to your contributions at any time with no taxes or penalties! That's right—you don't have to wait until age fifty-nine and a half to access your money in a Roth IRA. The capital gains (also called "profits" or "earnings"), on the other hand, can be withdrawn tax-free only after you turn fifty-nine and a half, or in a few instances in which the IRS makes an exception. These exceptions allow you to access capital gains before age fifty-nine and a half. For example, if you open a Roth IRA and fund it for five years, you're then allowed to withdraw up to $10,000 of gains for a first-time home purchase with zero taxes or penalties. That's on top of your ability to withdraw your contributions, so it's a pretty nice perk!

You can also use Roth IRA gains to pay for qualified education expenses, like college tuition. Gains used for this are taxed as income, but there are no penalty charges. These perks come with some drawbacks, such as not being able to deduct contributions from your taxable income when you file taxes the following year. For example, if your taxable income for 2023 was $16,500 and you contributed $6,500 to a Roth IRA in that year, you're not able to lower your tax bill with those contributions when you file taxes by April 2024. On the bright side, since the money you deposit into a Roth IRA was already taxed when you earned it, you'll never be taxed on it again.

One of the most powerful things about having a Roth IRA is that it's the only retirement account that doesn't require you to begin withdrawing money when you turn seventy-two. This is a called a "required minimum distribution" (RMD). Since you don't have to withdraw money unless you want to, the Roth IRA is the perfect account for passing down generational wealth. Anyone who inherits a Roth IRA never has to pay taxes on it, and that's a game changer! If you end up having enough money from other streams of income in retirement and don't need to tap your Roth IRA, you don't have to! You can name a beneficiary on the account and pass it down as tax-free generational wealth. Now, that's a flex!

These are some of the reasons the Roth IRA is my absolute favorite investment account, but there are also a few drawbacks to know about. For example, there's a limit on how much you can contribute each year. This annual limit changes from time to time, so it's important to always double-check the current maximum contribution limit on the IRS website for the most reliable information. It's typically several thousands of dollars. This maximum contribution is considered the total maximum for all of your Roth IRAs and traditional IRAs combined.

In 2023, the IRS updated the IRA contribution limit to $6,500 total. You could put $3,250 in a Roth IRA and $3,250 in a traditional IRA, or you could choose any other combination that adds up to $6,500 as long as you don't surpass it. If you contribute too much, you have to pay a penalty tax every year that it goes uncorrected! Ouch.

There are also income limitations to contributing to a Roth IRA, so not everyone is eligible for this type of retirement account. If you're a high-income earner, you won't be able to deposit money directly into the account, but there's a tax loophole called the "backdoor Roth IRA." The tax laws say high-income earners cannot contribute to a Roth IRA, but they don't say anything about *converting* to a Roth IRA!

Once you make too much income to qualify for contributions, you can open a traditional IRA instead and make a one-time contribution—preferably of the maximum contribution allowed—then immediately convert that account to a Roth IRA by selecting the "Roth IRA conversion" option in your account settings. Download your free guide at mindyourmoneybook.com for a step-by-step checklist to help with the backdoor Roth IRA strategy as well as details about one other important rule you must follow—the pro-rata rule. This rule applies anytime you convert money from a traditional IRA to a Roth IRA. You only need to worry about this if you plan to complete a Roth conversion, or a backdoor Roth IRA starting with a traditional IRA that already has contributions inside. This rule exists because pre-tax money invested in a traditional IRA cannot be converted to a Roth IRA without being taxed.

HUMANS VERSUS COMPUTERS

If you don't feel confident choosing your own investment accounts and investments, it may be a good idea to choose a robo-advisor or a financial advisor you can work with to create a plan.

The first time I invested outside of my 403(b) was when I opened an account with a robo-advising app called Betterment. I answered a few questions, and the algorithm immediately spit out a recommendation for me. A chart showed me the exact amount I'd have to invest in order to reach my goal. It also broke down what percentage of my contributions would buy equity ETFs versus bond ETFs. If I didn't want to pay the annual fee of 0.25 percent, I could have just opened my own account at a traditional brokerage firm and manually bought the ETFs they picked out for me.

At that time, I didn't know anything about investing. As a total newbie, it was nice to have it all done for me at once. When you work with a computerized platform or app that offers investing guidance and helps you get the account set up and funded, you pay an annual fee or management fee. This is significantly less than the fee you would pay to work with a human financial advisor, who collects information about you and gives you individualized investing guidance.

Financial advisors charge flat fees or a percentage of your account balance on a yearly basis. Those who charge a flat fee tend to charge several thousands of dollars per year, while those who charge a percentage range from charging 0.5 percent to 1 percent. These fees may also vary based on your account balance. The more you invest, the less you tend to pay in fees.

When people ask me whether or not they should work with a financial advisor, I first ask them this: Can you invest on your own using what you know about your time horizon, the 25x rule, diversifying through ETFs and index funds, and asset allocation? If you cannot, then you should seek help from a financial advisor or use a robo-advisor. If you feel confident that you can do it on your own, then ask yourself this: Do you know for a fact you can stomach stock market drops when bear markets come and decrease your account balance, or will you freak out and sell investments to cash out the bit you have left? If you cannot stomach volatility and know you'll sell in a panic, then it's worth it to have an advisor talk you through it and convince you not to sell when you panic. The key to being a successful investor over the long term is continuing to contribute to your accounts no matter what and sticking to your investment plan even when the market drops!

I often think that if Papi and Mami had known about IRA accounts, they could have retired with a very different standard of living. That's why I'm so obsessed with helping people learn about the benefits of these accounts. I know firsthand the difference they can make in your life. A few years before Papi retired, my siblings and I came together for a serious meeting because he didn't have enough money to stop working and he was approaching seventy!

Papi worked unforgiving jobs—washing dishes, baking, cooking at large restaurants, and eventually driving a taxi. He never worked a traditional job that offered him a 401(k) plan. Luckily, he has nine children who care for him and were willing to step in financially. My siblings and I set up a monthly savings fund to which we each contributed what we could. We did this for years before Papi retired to support him with paying rent, buying groceries, and covering other bills.

Of course, I'm the sibling who was put in charge of managing the account and paying the bills. You already know how I set things up! A high-yield savings account holds the funds we want to grow because the time horizon is immediate. My parents are both over age sixty-five, so we can't risk putting funds in the stock market. I also set up a checking account to put all the bills on autopay. Mami and Papi don't have to worry about paying the bills or the rent, they simply need to shop for groceries.

I helped my parents apply for Social Security benefits, but sadly, Mami didn't meet the 40 credits required by the Social Security Administration because she had been a stay-at-home mom. To earn credits, you need to work and pay Social Security taxes. After doing a bit of research, I helped her apply for spousal benefits, and she was approved for an amount equal to half of the monthly payment Papi gets.

Throughout this process, we learned that the Social Security Administration stopped mailing checks in 2013 and since then has shifted to an entirely digital process. I helped my parents open online bank accounts for the first time, and link their debit cards to their application for Social Security benefits. All of this was incredibly eye-opening for me! That's part of the reason I believe you need to start investing for retirement the moment you get your first paycheck. You deserve to retire with dignity. Generational wealth takes at least a generation. Go build wealth patiently, but aggressively.

CONCLUSION

Break the Cycle

MY PARENTS CAME TO THIS COUNTRY WITH ALMOST nothing and created a beautiful family of successful children and grandchildren. I'm beyond proud of how far they've come from their childhood experiences in rural Dominican Republic. While they were unprepared for retirement, I know it wasn't their fault. They did the best they could with the knowledge they had. Now that I've had the chance to learn what my parents never did, I won't ever take it for granted. With more knowledge, more access, and more opportunity, there's no excuse for us to not end old generational cycles and create new ones.

Improving your finances doesn't have to mean making huge, mind-blowing changes. It can actually be small steps you take to improve upon what you're already doing and get you where you want to be. You need determination and consistency, but most important, you need the courage to try new things that will challenge you. It takes tremendous courage to reach out and grab the life you want, but you already have what it takes! You didn't get to where you are today without tapping into courage.

Courage might mean changing banks for the first time in years. Maybe it's adding up all the debt you owe and facing your numbers head-on, or emailing your employer's HR manager to increase your 401(k) contributions by 1 percent.

No one accomplishes anything great alone. When you start working to improve your financial life, don't forget to ask for support and encouragement from others. Finding your tribe can make your financial transformation go much more smoothly. Ultimately, though, you have to take action right away. Don't finish this book and move on feeling awesome but then not act on those feelings. Rather than push your financial glow-up into the future, which might make you feel like you'll never get there, start *right now* with one action step from this book.

Here's a list of my key takeaways from each chapter to help you choose which you want to focus on first:

1. Commit to changing your financial life.
2. Turn scientific research into action.
3. Know the fundamentals of banking.
4. Follow the credit syllabus to get the credit score you deserve.
5. Create a debt payoff plan that includes failure on your path to success.
6. Set up your anti-budget, and put it on autopilot.
7. Invest in the greatest generator of wealth in history: the stock market.

Before publishing this book, I spoke at a Wealth and Wellness Retreat for entrepreneurial women of color. After my workshop, one of the women took to the stage and shared what she learned from me. Her key takeaway was that she no longer needs to operate in shame. As a licensed clinical psychologist, she felt confident in her emotional health, spiritual wellness, and even her physical health, but financial health had terrified her for years. She never wanted to talk about it and preferred to "stick her head in the sand." Tears ran down my face when she shared that I broke her out of the funk she had been stuck in with my joy and genuine compassion. She could hear me teach financial concepts and not feel like she was being convicted or condemned. Her parents, like mine, never learned the basics of financial literacy and she just needed to learn this stuff.

My hope is that you feel the same way now that you've reached the end of this book. I'm so freaking proud of you for making it this far. I sincerely hope this is just the beginning of an incredible journey for you, and I encourage you to share it with as many others as you can.

As for me, I'm tackling a big, hairy, audacious goal of my own: getting personal finance to be a standalone semester class requirement for high school graduation in all fifty states. In 2021, I began working as an advocate and I've since traveled to many states to testify in support of proposed legislation that would guarantee every student access to a class about personal finances. Getting my money right was so empowering and life-changing, but it doesn't end with me. This is about creating a legacy.

Whether I'm screaming about welfare in Mami's backyard, ranting about high-yield savings accounts on YouTube, advocating for lawmakers to include financial literacy in our public education system, or writing this book, I can't stop talking about money, and you shouldn't either!

Most self-help books focus on what you can do for you, and there's nothing wrong with that. But I want you to consider this book a "help others" book. Once you feel empowered with knowledge and tools to improve your own financial life, you've got to spread the wealth!

Host a *Mind Your Money* book club in your community! Gift this book to a friend, family member, or coworker. Buy a few copies for your local public school or library. Post about what you've learned on social media. Make sure you tag me @missbehelpful on all platforms so I can cheer you on and see how you're taking action.

Taking action is the number one, most important next step.

How dare we pretend to never have learned the wise words of Dr. Maya Angelou: "Do the best you can until you know better. Then when you know better, do better."

Printed in the USA
CPSIA information can be obtained
at www.ICGtesting.com
LVHW041918190923
758684LV00002B/293